PERSONAL BEST

The *Campus Life* Guide to Knowing and Liking Yourself

by DIANE EBLE

A DIVISION OF CTi
CampusLife
B O O K S

ZondervanPublishingHouse
Grand Rapids, Michigan
A Division of HarperCollins*Publishers*

Personal Best
Copyright © 1991 by Campus Life Books, a division of CTi
All rights reserved

Published by Zondervan Publishing House
1415 Lake Drive, S.E., Grand Rapids, Michigan 49506

Library of Congress Cataloging-in-Publication Data

Personal Best / [edited by] Diane Eble.
    p. cm.
    Summary: A guide for high school students discussing
how to develop one's self-esteem and identity, from a
Christian perspective.
    ISBN 0-310-71141-X
    1. Teenagers—Religious life. 2. Identification
(Religion)—Juvenile literature. 3. Self-respect—Religious
aspects—Christianity—Juvenile literature. [1. Identity.
2. Self-respect. 3. Christian life.] I. Eble, Diane, ill.
BV4850.P43   1991
248.8'3—dc20   90-26397
                             CIP
                             AC

Printed in the United States of America

91 92 93 94 95 / CH / 5 4 3 2 1

CONTENTS

About the YOUTHSOURCE™ Publishing Group

YOUTHSOURCE™ books, tapes, videos, and other resources pool the expertise of three of the finest youth-ministry resource providers in the world:

Campus Life Books—publishers of the award-winning *Campus Life* magazine, for nearly fifty years helping high schoolers live Christian lives.

Youth Specialties—serving ministers to middle-school, junior-high, and high-school youth for over twenty years through books, magazines, and training events such as the National Youth Workers Convention.

Zondervan Publishing House—one of the oldest, largest, and most respected evangelical Christian publishers in the world.

Campus Life	**Youth Specialties**	**Zondervan**
465 Gundersen Dr.	1224 Greenfield Dr.	1415 Lake Dr., S.E.
Carol Stream, IL 60188	El Cajon, CA 92021	Grand Rapids, MI 49506
708/260-6200	619/440-2333	616/698-6900

Introduction

This is a book about answering the questions, Who am I? How am I like other people? How am I different? What makes me unique? Where am I going?

It will help you to form a picture of yourself, a truer picture than you have now. Many people have a fuzzy image of themselves. If asked to describe their personalities, they come up with vague generalities. How can people be true to themselves if they don't really know who they are?

This process of defining yourself, of figuring out who you really are, never will be settled once and for all. It is a process that will continue all of your life. As new challenges confront you, you will fine-tune this internal sense of who you are. So why even bother? Well, because the better your sense of who you are, the better equipped you will be to meet the inescapable stresses and challenges of life. Quite simply, when you have a strong sense of identity you are a strong person. The pressures of life may be intense, but you will have an internal sense of identity to counterbalance the pressure from outside.

This book will start you on a journey, a quest for a definition of yourself. You will look at four major aspects of being human. Part One discusses the mental and emotional aspects, helping you get in touch with your feelings, thoughts, dreams, interests, and personality. Part Two focuses on the physical, exploring how you feel about your body. Part Three concentrates on the social realm, examining how others see you, who you become around your friends, and how the images other people hold up to you affect your own self-image. Finally, Part Four explores the spiritual dynamic of what you believe and value—your relationship with God, and how it is the foundation for your whole sense of who you are and where you are going.

By the time you finish this book, you should have a strong basis for defining yourself by God's Word and by the truth of your own experiences. You should be able to put into perspective the definitions pushed at you by society, the media, your peers, and your family. You will have a sharper, more accurate mental picture of the kind of person you are—and the person you are becoming.

Section One

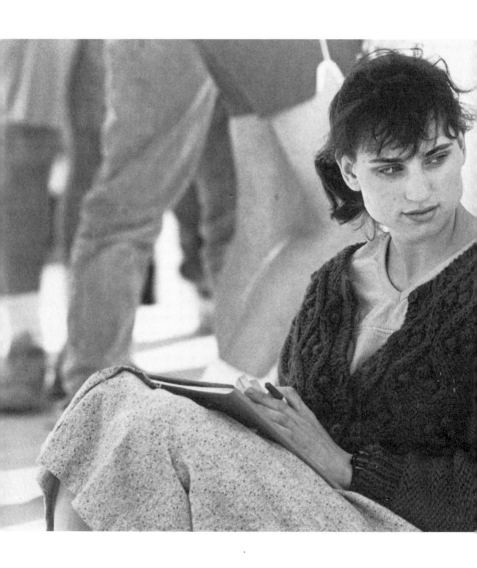

Mental/
Emotional

To be nobody but yourself in a world that is doing its best, night and day, to make you like everybody else, means to fight the hardest battle any human being can fight, and never stop fighting.

(e. e. cummings)

Loving and Hating Your Own Image

"Define yourself." It sounds like an exercise for dictionary makers, rather abstract and scientific.

Yet, when you try to define yourself you must begin at a very unscientific point—your emotions: Love. Hate. Fear. Joy.

You are, to yourself, like the closest friend you've ever had. Only closer.

You are, to yourself, like the biggest pest you've ever known. Only you can't escape this nuisance, even in your sleep.

When you live as close to someone as you do to yourself, you develop strong feelings about that person. Those little habits nobody else notices can drive you crazy. You tell yourself, *If he does that one more time I'll scream!*

On the other hand, living this close to someone can build deep feelings of affection and loyalty. Think of a dog who never leaves his master's side. Even though they're of different species, they become emotionally attached. So you, in some sense, are emotionally attached to yourself.

Start reading the "Your Turn" section and begin formulating your self-description. Try to use cold, objective facts, but be willing to express both love and hatred—the way you really feel about yourself.

YOUR TURN

Images of Me

If I were to draw a picture of myself, I would use

_X_ watercolors   ____ bold lines and shapes
____ oils   _X_ soft lines and shapes
____ pencil   ____ wild lines and shapes
____ poster paint   ____ controlled lines
____ charcoal   ____ other: _____
____ other: _____

_X_ my face alone   ____ dark colors
____ my body in motion   ____ bright colors
____ my body sitting still   _X_ pastel colors
____ myself with others   ____ earth tones
____ other: _____   ____ other: _____

What else would be included in your picture?

_____

Which feelings dominate—the positive or the negative? _____

Looking at your picture, would someone say you love yourself, hate yourself, or what?

I would say that they would feel "like" myself

Images of Me

If I could express myself in a verbal image, I would be (For instance: a dry leaf; a mysterious cat; a high-flying kite.)

1. _____

2. _____

3. _____

4. _____

5. _____

Which feelings dominate—the positive or the negative?

_____

_____

My favorite songs of all time:

	Theme:	**Emotion:**
1. *On my own*	*unrequitted love*	*heart-break*

2. _____ _____ _____

3. _____ _____ _____

4. _____ _____ _____

5. _____ _____ _____

Which feelings dominate? (Circle one from each pair.)

sad/happy   mellow/driving   involved/detached

peaceful/angry   excitement/boredom   celebration/gloom

fearful/hopeful   humorous/serious

I Hate Myself

An Anonymous Letter

I hate myself. I can't remember ever actually thinking, *I really like me.* Sometimes I get very depressed about it. I really wish I could go tell someone, talk to someone besides God about it.

Sometimes when I get depressed I start to list reasons why I hate myself:

1. *I'm ugly.* I go to a school where nearly all my friends are really cute. I have bad allergies, so I always have dark circles beneath my eyes. I don't have even close to a flawless complexion.

2. *I'm fat.* I do really need to lose weight, and having a younger sister who is much skinnier, more popular, and prettier than I am doesn't make things easier.

3. *I have no personality.* Sometimes I really wonder who I am. I know people say, "Just be yourself." But I have no idea who myself is. I've tried to be funny, serious, always smiling, a good listener, and more. I just don't know which I really am. How can I find me? Please don't tell me I'm just going through an identity crisis. I can remember having these thoughts since I was in the fourth grade.

4. *I'm stupid.* I'm not stupid in terms of intelligence; I make pretty good grades. I'm stupid in common sense. I'm a real dork and people kid me about it all the time.

5. *I have no real close friends.* No one would even notice if I died. I went to the same school for eight years and still felt that I didn't have a group of friends or fit in, so I changed schools to see if it was the school or me. It must be me, because after four months

in this new school I haven't begun to fit in here either. Now I truly feel that I don't belong anywhere.

I often think about dying. I even tried to commit suicide when I was about ten, but no one ever knew. Why shouldn't I die? I am miserable living like this. I don't want to commit suicide now, only because I know my family does care and it would hurt them. Still I pray all the time that God will let me die. I'm not at all afraid of death. I know I'm a born-again Christian and if I die I will finally be happy. There is nothing to lose.

After thinking about these things, which I often do, I feel terribly guilty. Do other people think about these things? As far as I can see, I have nothing to offer to the world around me.

I Love Myself

Marshall Norfolk

It starts with the sudden buzz of an alarm clock, this daily process of loving myself. I stagger to the bathroom, cup water in my hands, and splash my face, letting the water trickle between my fingers and dive off my chin into the sink. It takes me about forty minutes each day to prepare for the world by showering, grooming, and dressing.

That is 250 hours a year I spend getting ready to impress people. During the day, walking through the halls at school, I wonder whether I passed the test. *Are my clothes right? Do I fit in? Is my tan even? Do people notice me?* That's the main question. I certainly notice myself. It's as if I'm the only person who really matters. To me the others are shadow people who scurry through vague, less-than-real lives.

How do I love me? I begin by thinking about myself every waking moment of the day. My whole life is a strung-together collection of movie scenes, with me at the center of each one, playing the lead.

I think I love myself most when I'm with others. When I meet someone suave and successful who attracts people with his good looks and smooth style, something inside me clicks. I immediately start picking him apart, cutting him down: *Who does he think he is?* On the other hand, when I'm the center of attention, when it's my jokes people are laughing at, that's perfectly fair. I'm always first to congratulate myself on any success, like an award at school or a decent grade. It's OK for the spotlight to be trained on me; I just don't like someone else usurping my place.

Sometimes I blow it. I'll say something crude. Or miss an easy pass. Or flunk a test. Even then, while on the outside I'm hot with embarrassment and anger, inside I'm making excuses, rationalizing my failure away. *It's my parents' fault for being too demanding and nosy . . . The sun blinded me . . . My teachers have no compassion.*

In any argument, my cause is the right one. If my parents insist on their way, I'll grudgingly concede, but then punish them by withdrawing and sulking. *They don't trust me,* I grouse.

I trust myself, always.

I love myself.

Once I had a frightening thought. What if my sister, my mother, my teachers—everyone in the world—loved themselves in the same way I love myself? What if they glossed over their flaws and magnified their good points just as I did? Would the world go crazy, with all those egotists walking around?

Then the suspicion hit me. Could it be they *do* consider themselves just as important as I consider myself? The thought frightened me, because it hit me so suddenly that I have never considered for a moment what it would be like to be them. I've been too intent on loving myself to jump the gap and see the world through their eyes. Other people have been characters in *my* movie. But what about their movies, in which I play but a minor part—how do I look there?

Jesus told a very successful, cocky man that the way to live right is to "love your neighbor as yourself" (Luke 10:27). I know how I love myself. It's the main preoccupation of my life—my first thought in the morning, my last at night. I've hardly considered loving others in the same way. I have never helped them by praising their good traits and forgiving their mistakes the way I want people to respond to me. It's much easier to block them off, to continue seeing them as minor characters in my life, undeserving even of a credit line.

What would happen if I truly loved them as I love myself?

YOUR TURN

I love me, I love me not, I love me, I love me not. Which of the preceding people did you relate to most? Chances are, you related to both of them in some ways. All of us have some things we hate about ourselves. We hate our pimples, our height, our shyness, our nose, the way we laugh—the list can be long.

At the same time, we take good care of ourselves. We are aware of our flaws, and we spend lots of energy glossing over them so that other people won't notice.

It's a paradox. We love ourselves, we hate ourselves. And it's OK. Part of learning to be ourselves is to accept the fact that we are a number of contradictory things all at the same time.

You are selfish and compassionate, sensitive and indifferent, friendly and snobbish, fearful and courageous. You want to belong to the crowd, yet to be your own person; to be independent from your folks, yet secure in their love; to be attractive to the opposite sex, yet admired for who you are rather than what you look like.

The thoughts that flit through your mind probably are like the thoughts many people have—yet no one else will ever think of blue skies when they smell a certain perfume like you do. Everyone has felt nervous, excited, anxious, and on top of the world—but no one has ever felt them in quite the same combination as you did on your first date. No one has the same set of fingerprints as you, nor the same combination of shape, height, and coloring. Most important, no one else has the same relationship with God, the one who made you and knows you clear through to the bone.

PERSONAL BEST

Learning to be you means accepting your own uniqueness, contradictions and all, and using it as a point of growth for yourself. Learning to be you means finding out what you have to give to others and to the world.

But what if you don't know who you are or don't like who you are? What if you're like Louie, the next person to introduce herself in this book?

Louie

Lois Breiner

When I was a kid, I hated myself for being a girl. I wore jeans, an old shirt, and a baseball cap whenever I could. As early as five years old I swaggered around town and spit in the street. At seven I insisted everyone call me Louie and wouldn't answer them unless they did.

All through elementary school I was a tomboy. "Can't I *ever* be a boy?" I whined to my parents.

"Be proud you're a girl," they scolded.

Proud of it? Never! At least the boys accepted me during those years. I never wanted to play with the sissy girls. Sometimes I had to play with my girl cousins, who only wanted to play house. I broke up housekeeping pretty quickly one time by throwing around all the dishes and pans. Then I climbed into a tree and bombed the other girls with rocks.

Right through sixth grade I fought anybody. The teachers warned me about playing too roughly. "That's no way for a little *lady* to act," they'd cluck.

"I'm no lady!" I'd bark, spitting for emphasis and wiping my nose on my sleeve.

But in seventh grade, the boys didn't want me around anymore. I couldn't understand why. Neither could they, except that for some reason it was totally uncool to have a girl in their group. They dismissed me from all games with, "Aw, you play like a girl." That wasn't true; I could run, pitch, and tackle as well as the next guy.

When the boys rejected me, I started hanging around with the girls. I figured I could tolerate it. In fact, I found out I liked it. I gradually discovered there were some nice things about being a girl. As the years passed, my femininity emerged. Yet, I still wanted to be anybody but me.

There was a time halfway between wanting to be a boy and wanting to be a girl when I was really worried. I *was* a girl; where did the tomboy feelings come from? What if I *always* wanted to be a boy? Had my genes and chromosomes united in some kind of freak pattern?

But that wasn't the trouble. The tomboy problem was just on the surface; the deeper problem was that I wanted to be anybody but me. I didn't like myself. Whatever was "un-me"—being a boy and not a girl, being smooth and confident instead of self-conscious—was the attractive thing. *The real me*, I thought, *wasn't all that valuable.*

Eventually I tried to build another character and create another personality inside. I went at it with as much determination as I'd used trying to be a boy. I borrowed the qualities of anybody I admired, using them as building blocks to construct the "new me." I thought people around me had a lot more going for them than I did. I tried to adopt the personalities of successful characters in books and movies. I tried to be free and confident like Julie Andrews, or sophisticated and dramatic like Liz Taylor, or tragic but optimistic like Jane Eyre. Pretty soon I wasn't sure which parts of myself were real and which parts were copied from others.

But one thing was certain, I wasn't really me. I was a mixture of somebody else trying to fit in, trying to say and do the right things and wear what everyone else was wearing. I had no idea what *I* thought, felt, valued, or believed in.

Then one day I heard, for the first time, that God accepts us the way we are. He doesn't demand that we think or act or talk like anybody else. Those thoughts sank slowly in. God had made me a valuable, unique individual. He wanted me to be 100 percent me—shy or outgoing, funny or serious, flashy or steady and dependable. Whatever "me" was, that's what God wanted.

It wasn't always easy to face myself in those terms. There was a lot of "me" I didn't like at all. I hated my sense of humor, because I thought it blew my image as a deep, serious thinker. Now I discovered that being able to make others laugh was a great way to put them at ease or cheer them up. I had always kept my opinions to myself, afraid of seeming stupid. Now I found that when I spoke, people really listened to what I had to say.

Instead of dwelling on my weak points, I began to look at the positive. I started to see I wasn't so bad, that I was a person worth knowing.

Unfortunately those thoughts didn't sink deep enough. Instead of asking Christ to help me find myself, I took full charge of the job. After a while, my inward search became a hassle.

Frustrated, I crept back to my old ways and began rebuilding another self. I figured I was older, more experienced—the person I'd create could be better. But one day those thoughts about God suddenly took a much deeper hold. I discovered Jesus Christ, and he lit up my real self all the way down to the basement.

When Jesus introduced me to myself, I began to feel a lot happier and more comfortable. The friendships I formed were deeper. With Jesus I could be more me, someone I liked better than anyone I'd ever tried to be.

The transformation has taken time. I didn't immediately like myself; there were times when I still tried to act as I thought a cool person should. In fact, I still do. But my goal is set: I'm going to be me, the person Christ made me to be, with all my quirks. If that's all he wants me to do, it's all I want as well.

YOUR TURN

Learning to be the real you. Do you know the real you? Or do you find yourself, like Lois Breiner, trying to adopt the personality traits of people you admire? How do you know who "the real you" is anyhow? To start to find out, work on these lists.

WHAT I LIKE ABOUT MYSELF:

I am sensitive, I love art (i.e drama)

WHAT I DON'T LIKE ABOUT MYSELF:

self concious (too sensitive)

Once you've written down everything you can think of, circle any traits that seem "borrowed" and not fully you.

For the negative traits, underline those that could be considered positive, given the right context. (For instance, seriousness.)

What to Do with What You Don't Like

It's good to begin seeing the positive side to many negatives. But you're probably still left with some negative aspects of yourself in which you can see no good whatsoever. Think about these traits as you read the following article. Here, six kids talk to Dave Carlson, a social worker at Trinity College in Deerfield, Illinois, about what it feels like inside their shells.

Ron: My problem is I give up too easily. I'd really like to be number one, but I never am. I succeed just enough to get a taste of it, then I go through a period where I lose interest; I'd rather just go out with my friends and have a good time. By the time I'm in the mood to get back into it, I'm way behind. Like playing the violin. I really like to play and I wish I were excellent. I'm not, though, and that tends to depress me and keep me from working at it, which in turn keeps me from being very good. It's an endless cycle.

Dave: You remind me of a high jumper who jumps six feet and gives up because it's not the world's record. Suppose you were only five feet tall, and you high jumped six feet. You could either get discouraged because it wasn't a world-class jump, or you could be satisfied, realizing that with your height a jump of six feet is very good. It's a question of matching your abilities to your accomplishments. If you set goals that are simply unreachable, you'll end up frustrated. It sounds like you've done that. Then, because you see yourself as unsuccessful, you give up even sooner than you ought to. You need to figure out realistic goals.

Ron: That would be fine if I were just trying to please myself. But the standards in my high school are fierce. If you're not a total success, you're a flop.

Dave: It's not just your high school. Our whole culture says you have to be a winner. The trouble is, there can be only one winner. Everybody else is a loser. To pretend everybody can be a winner is devastating. So what if you're number two in something? You need to realize that someone is number 349. Paul says in Galatians that we should do our very best, not compare ourselves with other people.

I see the competition game in college freshmen a lot. They come with the idea everybody's got to be a straight-A student, and they forget that there probably aren't ten straight-A students on a whole campus. They're setting themselves up for a big fall.

Ron: But even when I have realistic goals, I get tired of going after them. How can I make my motivation consistent?

Dave: Really, this fits in with making realistic goals. If you never calculate on a few emotional ups and downs, you're in for trouble. You said before that when you get tired of chasing success, you go out with your friends and have a good time. There's nothing wrong with that. We all need our escapes. That's what weekends are for. They let the pressure off—give us time to lick our wounds.

Mostly it's a question of evaluating what's really important in light of what Christ taught. Study the Bible to see Christ's priorities. Maybe the things you're pursuing aren't all that important. If going out with your friends and having a good time is important to you, stop kicking yourself for it. You can't do everything.

Steve: My problem isn't performance—it's something I can't help. I have a gross case of acne and it really bugs me.

Dave: Well, I hardly need to say that you should check it out with a doctor if you haven't already. There aren't any easy answers for people with skin problems, because in our society these people are labeled undesirable. Take it a step further. What if you had a birthmark or scar on your face that wouldn't ever go away?

Think about how people really react to you. There are plenty of kids who have skin problems *and* lots of friends. You may be mentally exaggerating its effect on other people. In fact, you may be so sensitive that your attitude is what's creating the problem, not your face. If something can't be changed, you've got to accept it.

It's true, though, that accepting something the world considers ugly doesn't happen overnight. I have a friend with rheumatoid arthritis. She's had it her entire forty-year life, but she still can't totally accept her deformed body and she has periods of depression. There are things about ourselves we'll never be able to accept entirely, like our level of intelligence, the way we look, physical deformities, the fact that we are adopted or a foster child, or whatever. These things can upset you periodically throughout your life.

From a Christian perspective you should know you're lovable, regardless of what you look like. God loves you, and that's the basic standard for values. To accept that is very, very crucial.

Learn to thank God for who you are and for the circumstances he's given you. I don't mean you should thank God mindlessly, ignoring your real feelings. Read the Psalms and see how David prayed. He really got angry with God at times, yet in the middle of that he still thanked him. Praising God should be the result of getting in touch with all your feelings of depression and anger and sadness, then saying, "Lord, in spite of what's going on, I've come to the place where I can say, 'Praise your holy name.' I am angry and hurt about these things, but I know you are the One who is in control. I want to reaffirm that fact with you, and thank you for it."

Robin: I'm shy. Who knows why? But I hate nothing more than confronting a roomful of strangers. I feel I could never lead at anything. How can I change?

Dave: What you can do depends a lot on why you're shy. Maybe your family is just quiet. I'd sit down and figure out what circumstances you *do* feel comfortable in, and work from there. Find jobs you feel secure in, but that also force you out of yourself.

Usually people aren't shy for no reason. I'm a great believer in finding out what causes your shyness and dealing with that. Finding a competent older person to talk to can help.

Whatever you do, remember you don't change yourself

overnight. First you have to figure out what kind of person you really want to be, then find ways of becoming that person. Finally, you have to endure the long, sometimes painful process of change. If you want to stop being shy, it will cost something. You will have to stick your neck out. It can be a very gradual change, but you still have to evaluate the cost and ask yourself, "Is it worth it?"

Plenty of people go through life shy, and there's nothing wrong with that as long as it's what they want to be. As Paul said, "There are many ways in which God works in our lives, but it is the same God who does the work in and through all of us who are his" (1 Cor. 12:6 LB). God loves variety. That's why he made us all different—for him.

Sue: I guess I'm different from Robin. I have a lot of friends; I'm a cheerleader, and I talk a lot. Sometimes I think I talk too much. I'm sure nobody thinks I have a problem in the world. But the truth is I feel very insecure. I wonder whether the guys who take me out really care about me. That goes for all my friends, too. Would they still like me if they really knew me? I don't want to feel this way, but I do.

Dave: You know, half the problem with feeling this way is that you probably think you're the only one to have these feelings. But you aren't. Lots of people who look like they've got things together are really all confused inside. I wish you and Robin would sit down together and talk about this, because it would probably help Robin to know you share a lot of her problems. And you probably need to talk about your feelings with some of your friends. Ask them if they've ever felt this way and how they solved it. I'll bet some of them feel very much like you do. Getting it out in the open will help.

These problems may go deeper, though. How do the important people in your life treat you? If your parents and teachers jump on you, it's easy to start jumping on yourself. If that's where your insecure feelings are coming from, you'll have to solve that problem first. Get to the source of the problem! Doing anything else is like bailing water to fix a still-broken water main. You have to fix the leak before you start bailing.

Paul: That last thing you said to Sue, that's exactly my problem. I really lack confidence, and the reason is my brothers and sisters are always putting me down. They make me feel I'm worthless, and consequently I don't do as well at things as I should. Like last year—I quit basketball the first day of practice. I said it was because it was too much work, but actually I was afraid I wouldn't make it.

Dave: I wouldn't jump to the conclusion that it's all your brothers' and sisters' fault. Are you doing something that leads them on? For instance, you may be acting like a self-righteous goody-goody who gets them in trouble and comes out smelling like a rose yourself. If you're earning their criticism, you need to change. Maybe talking to your brothers and sisters would help.

Then consider how you handle the put-downs. Do you attack back and escalate the problem? Or do you just walk away and forget it? There are things you can do that defuse criticism instead of adding to it. Make a joke out of it, or ask them for some specific actions you can take to improve.

Finally, this may be a situation that isn't your fault at all. Maybe you're like Joseph in the Old Testament, whose parents were especially fond of him and neglected the other kids. It isn't surprising that the neglected kids grow to resent situations like that. It might be that you are an innocent victim. If the situation isn't your fault and is beyond your control, perhaps you can go and talk to your parents about the whole thing.

Richard: I'm a good tennis player. I really want to be good, so I do the things I know are necessary. I practice maybe four to five hours a day, and I always play guys who are better than I am. But when I make mistakes, it really bugs me. People around here love to laugh at me. Sometimes I go home after playing and put on a record loud so that I don't have to think about myself, and I leave it on until I'm tired enough to sleep. There must be a better way to live with myself.

Dave: You remind me of Ron. You both really want to succeed and it sounds as if you both cringe at failure. But you've handled the problem in exactly the opposite way from Ron. Ron got discouraged and gave up when faced with his own mistakes. It sounds as if you just work harder.

I sense a lot of self-doubt. Do you mock yourself? Can you take a compliment? When someone says you did a good job, can you just say thank you, or do you have to put yourself down? You may need to learn to like yourself.

Setting realistic standards for yourself helps. The truth is most of us could do better. That's not something to get down on yourself for—it's the normal thing. You have to accept the fact that you're not going to be at 100 percent very often.

More than that. I'd encourage you to think out why you want to be such a good tennis player. Is it really worth the cost? If it is, work on it for all you're worth. But realize it is going to cut you off from other areas of life. Do you want it that badly? I'm a bogie golfer. If I don't get a par on every hole, I can give a million reasons why. But I have to be realistic about it. I can't expect to be a par golfer when I play three or four times a year. I have to say, "This is where I am, and it's OK." I don't care enough about golf to play every day—and that's fine.

There are things you can't change, but that doesn't mean you pretend it doesn't hurt. If you weren't born with good looks, it may hurt. Let it! Don't pretend you haven't lost something—you have! But after you've done your crying, accept it and move on with what you have. You don't have to be able to say, "I'm number one." It's enough before God to say, "I've done my best."

Strategies for Making Changes

Steve Lawhead

A lot of personal problems are related to deep-seated fears of such things as failure or rejection. What fear gnaws at you the most? What chills your eyeballs and turns your knees to jelly? What deep, dark fear lurks within you, ready to reduce your healthy frame to a pile of palpitating protoplasm?

OK, maybe your fears aren't that terrorizing, but we all have at least one secret (or maybe not-so-secret) fear, a looming dread that hangs like a black thundercloud and never fails to rain on our parade.

Whatever it is that rattles you, you're probably not alone. For instance, about 90 million Americans admit to being shy—that's close to half of the country's adult population!

Knowing others suffer with you is worth something. Still, such knowledge usually falls a wee bit short of making you feel genuinely grand about the situation. Most sufferers would rather stop the suffering than soak up sympathy.

Well, good news! There usually is a cure for what bugs you. The bad news is that the cure is costly in terms of hard work, determination, commitment, and willpower. Some people, when they find out how much it costs, decide being cured isn't worth the effort. But others want to search out an answer, no matter what the cost. "I don't care how expensive it is," they say, "I'm worth it." If you're one of those people, read on.

The ideas in this article will not automatically solve your problems. They will, however, put you through some planned paces that will provide strategies for getting your mind ready to trim your problem down to size. There are two approaches that, in varying degrees, help with anything from shyness to pogonophobia (the fear of beards). In laymen's terms, they might be called the "Kamikaze" and the "Assault on Everest."

THE KAMIKAZE

This technique is not recommended for the fainthearted, involving as it does a wild-eyed death leap into the very element one fears the most. You know, brutal confrontation, no holds barred, sink or swim—that sort of thing.

A kamikaze is one who hurls himself at his enemy in the blind hope of vanquishing him. Say you're afraid of mice. Using the Kamikaze method, you'd confront that fear in a dramatic way, such as loosing several hundred rodents in your bedroom and then spreading CheezWhiz on the soles of your feet. Who knows? Maybe by morning you would have conquered your fear.

Another example of the Kamikaze method might be a person who has a morbid fear of snakes locking himself in a cage with the critters. The idea is that if he can live through the ordeal he will no longer stand in terror when a garter snake crosses his path.

Theoretically, this "cure" works because of a simple, well-known fact of human nature: You fear what you do not know. By boldly confronting the object of your fear and facing the thing that stirs your apprehension, you remove its mystery. Once the aspect of the unknown is removed, you may no longer fear it because you know it. Or at least you may have an idea how to cope. The things you know well you no longer fear irrationally. They may never be your favorite things, but you are free of the uninformed phobia that once possessed you.

But what about deeper problems or fears? How do shyness and loneliness, for instance, fit into this discussion? They aren't fears, exactly, are they?

Well, they are and they aren't. You may not think of shyness or loneliness as a fear, but when they are traced to their roots you'll find they *are* well-grounded in fear.

Shyness is actually a collective term for a number of associated fears—sort of like a trade union: The UF & PASI—The

Union of Fears and Phobias Associated with Social Interaction. Fear of strangers, or members of the opposite sex, or large groups, or small intimate groups, or many other things, all are constituents of UF & PASI. A person who is shy is actually subscribing to one or more of these fears.

You could think of loneliness as another side of shyness in most cases. It often grows out of the same basic fears that feed shyness: the fear of rejection, chiefly, but also fear of ridicule, fear of intimacy, or fear of being vulnerable to another person. Shyness creates an atmosphere where loneliness can thrive. Shy people often are lonely people, and those who are lonely are shy and unable to let people ease their pain.

Suppose your shyness consists of a fear of the opposite sex. Using the Kamikaze method you'd muster your courage by whatever means possible and actually approach that cute guy or girl and *talk* to him or her, ask for a date, compare notes on geometry theorems, discuss your hypothesis that people get the weather they deserve . . . anything to get the conversation moving. If you are successful, you will find your fear has diminished—perhaps even vanished—because you actually talked to a guy or girl and you didn't die doing it. Your shyness may not simply walk away, but you probably will gain a surprising sense of progress that can even carry you through future fears.

Risky? Sure it is. That's why they call it the "Kamikaze," folks! Kamikazes risk certain death each time they go out. They don't plan on returning because they would rather die gallantly in the attempt than live with the shame of giving up. Desperate plans call for desperate measures. If you fail, fail big. Then dust off your pride and give it another go. Conversely, if you win—and often you *will* win—you win big. Either way, you've made a dent in the armor you figured was invincible.

However, if the Kamikaze seems a tad too extreme, perhaps the second approach is for you.

THE ASSAULT ON EVEREST

Prepare for a slow, steady upward climb to the summit of your particular mountain of fear.

Using the fear of snakes once again as an example, in the

Assault on Everest method you would not pull an Indiana Jones by throwing yourself into a pit with black mambas, cobras, and rattlers. Instead, you would plan a campaign that established base camps ever higher along the trail to the top.

First, you might go to the library, check out a book about snakes, and look at the pictures. Once you're comfortable with that you could go to a zoo and gaze at the real thing from behind the safety of three inches of tempered glass. When you could manage that without cringing (perhaps after several trips), you might go to a pet store and look at a specimen closely. Later you could ask the pet store owner to let you touch a snake while he holds it. For the final ascent to the summit, you might go with an experienced backpacker on a hike into snake territory with the purpose of viewing or photographing snakes in their natural habitat. When you are able to see them without screaming and/or fainting, you are cured!

Clearly, this method of dealing with phobias is less risky, and that is its appeal. You can progress at your own rate in controlled situations. You climb to the top slowly, moving from strength to strength.

The only problem is that this takes a concentrated effort sustained over a long period of time. Often that is discouraging in itself. But if conquering your fear is important to you, and the flaming plunge of the Kamikaze seems needlessly suicidal, then breaking your fear into manageable pieces and devouring them one small slice at a time is your best bet.

Many psychologists use this same approach with their phobia sufferers. One psychologist works with people who are afraid to fly. He starts them out watching films about flying, and then moves on to simulated flight with role playing. When they are secure with that, the aerophobes progress to boarding airplanes, and finally to taking a real trip via jet.

To deal with a shyness problem using this strategy, you might make speaking before a large group your goal and then design a series of steps (or base camps, à la the mountaineering motif) that lead up to it.

First, you might watch television programs, newscasts maybe, where people do a lot of public speaking. You could watch and reflect on what they were doing and how they did it. Then you might attend some city council meetings or speeches of local political candidates, taking notes on the various aspects of speech-making such as eye contact, voice projection, and gestures.

Next you might write a speech and practice it before a mirror. When you were comfortable with that, you might begin taking opportunities to speak in small-group settings—with friends over a Coke or in a small study group at school—anywhere two or three people are discussing something and you would have the opportunity to join in with your views. You might ask to address a small group on a topic you care about—lead a Bible study, for example—and keep at it until you were able to do that with dash and aplomb. Then it would be time to volunteer to narrate the Christmas program at church or give an oral book report to your English class.

WILL IT WORK?

"Sounds good in theory," you say, but will it help *me*?" Most likely, yes. The common, everyday, garden-variety problems usually respond nicely to these two techniques. Even such involved (though common) problems as shyness are more easily managed after using the Everest climb or Kamikaze attack.

You must realize, though, that you are in for some hard work—work that will demand the utmost determination and commitment. It may seem easier to cling to your fear than to try to conquer it because solutions require change—and change is one of the most difficult things a person can do.

But if you've had enough of your personal hassle and want to change, below are some tips to help point you in the right direction:

1. *Work at understanding yourself better.* Sit down in a quiet place and ask yourself *who* you are and *why.* Try to discover your overall strengths and weaknesses. What do you want to change?

2. *Work at understanding what is underlying the problem.* If you're acting or feeling a way you don't want to, it's probably because some fear is pushing you to it. Spend time, when you feel safe and secure, thinking about your fear. Why are you

afraid? What has happened in your life to make you afraid? Is it rational or irrational? How might you overcome it? Just toy with the idea of conquering your fear; try the idea on for size. Once you have a grasp on the nature of and reason for your fear, you'll be in a much better position to deal with it.

3. *Build your self-confidence.* Take what you've learned about yourself and your fear and use it to build a little self-confidence. You will easily find ways to bolster your ego now and then without having to stick your neck out too far. Work at affirming yourself when you do something right or when you see places where you could have been afraid but weren't. In this way you can build yourself up for the bigger change to come.

4. *Design a specific plan of attack.* Sit down with a pencil and paper and determine what you want to accomplish and possible ways to achieve it. Develop a step-by-step plan that you can follow to reach your goal. Whichever means you use— kamikaze or assault on Everest—you'll need a good plan. Don't rush this step. Take your time and examine it from all angles.

5. *Follow your plan.* When you feel confident in yourself and in your plan, do it. Pick a day, circle it on your calendar, make that D day, and do it! Become the kamikaze or set out on your climb. Don't allow yourself to back down. Remember what a wise man once said: "The only thing we have to fear is fear itself."

YOUR TURN

Problems as opportunities. If you haven't already done so, now is the time to follow the five steps Steve Lawhead suggested. Your end product: a plan for change in the areas of your life that you don't like.

What I'd Like to Change:

_____

Strategy Choice:

_____ Kamikaze

_____ Assault on Everest

Steps in My Plan:

1. _____

2. _____

3. _____

4. _____

5. _____

6. _____

A World with No Lonely People

Philip Yancey

Here's a thought to chew on mentally: What may initially appear to be a problem may actually be an opportunity in disguise. It may be an opportunity to grow in some new way— a chance to help someone else as only you, with your unique set of strengths and weaknesses and life experiences, can help.

The next article shows how very common problems, like loneliness and shyness, can be stepping-stones to personal growth and outreach.

Sometimes I yearn for a world without loneliness. What would it be like if we were all self-confident? If we didn't need people to smile at us and notice us? If we were all like perfect, rounded eggs, with a smile decal pasted on our faces?

And as I fantasize, I inevitably come back to a strange conclusion: Thank you, God, for loneliness.

Loneliness is not the sort of feeling that normally makes you thankful. There aren't accurate statistics on it (i.e., 3,475,212 people in America cried themselves to sleep last night because of loneliness), but it's safe to say that all of us feel lonely a good chunk of the time. Sometimes it goes away—when we're really connecting with friends, when we're loved, when our families are humming together like they're meant to. But always the gnawing feeling returns, eating away at us from the inside, causing us to wonder what is wrong with us since no one wants to be with us. It depresses us and corrodes our self-image.

Why, then, am I thankful for loneliness? Because it's the one thing within me that *forces* me to reach out to other people.

I think of three friends—Heather, Ralph, and Sharon. In each of their cases, loneliness had spread beyond the common-cold stage; it was a cancer. They needed me. I saw it. Yet in the back of my mind I thought, *Aha, I must be a better, more self-sufficient person then they are. I'm not that lonely. I don't need to stoop down and waste my time with people who can't cope.*

If only I had been lonelier, I might have been forced to reach out to them. If I had admitted my own loneliness more, I could perhaps have been their cure.

Loneliness is a magnet, just like sex. Because of sex, a married couple is brought together again and again, even when resentments pile up. Even when the hairline has receded and the midriff bulges over the belt and the *Glamour* figure is a blurred memory—still sex pulls a husband and wife together. It is a magnet.

So it is with loneliness. If we let it, it can be a magnet that pulls us to other people, even when we're laughed at, or excluded from a group, or insulted by sarcasm.

Don't deny your loneliness. Free it, then let it push you toward others. A Christian especially has an advantage because he has experienced Jesus, who promised, "I will never leave you nor forsake you." You can be a cure for others' loneliness. You have a source, a person will always care for you. God loves you as if you were the only one he had to love.

The Gospels ring with stories of Jesus' aloneness. He was misunderstood and not appreciated. Even with his twelve close friends—disciples who followed him wherever he went for three years and listened to everything he said—he was lonely. If you read the accounts of that heart-wrenching, emotional time right before Jesus' death (see Matt. 26:17–56), you can't help sensing Jesus' profound loneliness.

No one else understood what was happening or why. Jesus knew both, and he knew that one of his disciples would turn him over to the soldiers that night. Jesus went out to the Garden of Gethsemane to pray, taking his disciples with him, but they were so insensitive that they kept falling asleep. And, one by one, as it became clear their Master would be executed like a common criminal, they deserted him. Jesus faced death entirely alone.

Even Peter, Jesus' most outspoken friend, denied that he knew Jesus and cursed when asked if he was Jesus' disciple.

Jesus was all alone.

But there is a powerful scene in the last chapter of the book of John that shows how Jesus conquered loneliness. The disciples had withdrawn from their dreams of a kingdom and were at their old jobs, fishing in the early morning fog. But Jesus had not withdrawn from them. He went to find them, and when he did he called them over to him and served breakfast on the beach. There, in front of the others, he asked Peter the same piercing question three times: "Peter, do you love me?"

Imagine the pain Peter felt as he was forced to look into the eyes of the friend he had betrayed. And, as Peter answered yes each time, Jesus responded, "Then feed my sheep."

Peter got the message. He was to quit feeling sorry for himself and get on with the task of reaching out to others. He did so and became one of the most effective Christians in history.

Peter's example shows that the solution to our longing is not a world without lonely people, but a world of people who use their loneliness to reach out to others. There are two aspects. First, we must link up to God, who loves us and accepts us regardless of our failings. Every time we fail Jesus, he still stands there and asks, "Do you love me? If so, get on with the work of loving other people."

The second part of the solution to loneliness is the response of reaching out to others. God created us incomplete, not as a cruel trick to edge us toward self-pity but as an opportunity to edge us toward others with similar needs.

Jesus summarized his advice about relationships in one statement: "Do to others what you would have them do to you" (Matt. 7:12). Applied to the problem of loneliness, that could be restated: "Assume everyone else in the world is at least as lonely as you, then act toward them as you'd want them to act toward you."

YOUR TURN

Turn Your Scars into Stars

Can you recall any particular time when something you thought of as a negative trait—shyness, for example—actually turned into an opportunity for personal growth or for helping someone else? Write about it.

The quality I've regarded negatively is _____. Here's how it turned out for good:

_____

_____

_____

_____

_____

_____

CLASSIFYING THE NEGATIVES

Things I Don't Like About Myself and Plan to Change:

not being fit / eating habits

study skills

be always well groomed
organized

Things I Don't Like About Myself That Can Be Used for Good:

my fearfullness

Things I Don't Like, Can't Change, and Must Simply Accept:

my breakouts

Using this basic inventory you're ready for the next chapter, for now you know what you like and you know what you don't like. I also hope that you can begin to see yourself as a very special, one-of-a-kind person.

The One and Only You

It is an awesome thought that each of us is completely unique. Among all of the billions of people that have ever lived upon this earth there is no one just like you.

You are a rarity, a unique creation, an original that can't be copied.

The earth has never seen, nor ever will see, someone just like you.

You deserve to respect yourself as a creation so precious that you should want to develop all that has been given to you.

Each of us was given certain talents and abilities, some of them found only in us. These are to be developed and used to help and serve both ourselves and others. Or they can be used for self alone, or not at all.

Every time you deny these talents and your own uniqueness, or say you can't do something before you've tried, you're closing off some part of that room to the future.

Each time you put yourself down by comparing yourself unfavorably with others, you're copping out of life. (Barbara Varenhorst, *Real Friends*)

What makes you unique? Several things.

First, your feelings. They color your world, sometimes with harsh, dark tones, sometimes with soft and subtle hues. Being in touch with the full range of your emotions and responding to them appropriately puts you in touch with who you are in a powerful way.

Your personality makes you unique. Some people think personality is what makes certain people popular. The truth is that everyone has a personality, and a unique one at that. Affirming your unique personality frees you from wearing masks when you're around other people. (It also helps other people to like your unique personality.)

Your dreams are unique, too. They can shape your future— but they have to be more than mere fantasy. When they are combined with your interests, another factor in your uniqueness, your dreams can be the key to a fulfilling future that combines service to others with what you enjoy doing best.

Feelings: Understanding Them, Expressing Them

Steve and Alice Lawhead

Three minutes before the end of the state basketball championship game, Jim fouled out. The ref's call was questionable and the entire team protested, but Jim was sent to the bench anyway.

By the time he reached the sidelines, he was steaming.

"Did you see what they did to me?" Jim hollered at the coach.

"Forget it, Wilson. Sit down and cool off!"

"But Coach, he deliberately—"

"You heard me. Calm down or hit the showers!"

Wendy wanted to act. When tryouts for the school play were announced, Wendy secured a script and diligently studied it. She practiced whenever she could and memorized her lines without any problem.

But she froze at the audition. She flubbed several lines and got confused about stage directions. Worst of all, she was shocked to discover that she had to sing a song from the play—in front of everybody. She was so nervous that she had trouble hitting half of the notes and she forgot most of the words. She dashed from the stage before the song was ever finished.

Someone else got the part; Wendy didn't even make the chorus. She couldn't bear to go back to school—all she could think about was the horrible audition.

"Snap out of it, Wendy," her mother said. "It's not the end of the world."

* * *

Rick and David had been best friends since sixth grade. They did everything together. They signed up for the same classes, they studied together, and they both worked at Burger King. Rick dated Cindy, a girl from his church whom he liked a lot. David dated Sue, a friend of Cindy's.

One day Rick overheard Sue and Cindy talking about Cindy's date the night before, with *David*. Rick was stunned. He confronted David with the information.

"Sure, I went out with Cindy," David confessed. "Why? I just wanted to get to know her better. I knew you'd understand."

But Rick didn't understand. He wouldn't have anything to do with either David or Cindy after that. He spent his time plotting revenge.

"Quit overreacting," his father told him. "Be a man and get back in the game."

Emotions, especially powerful ones like anger and jealousy, can be pretty messy. It makes us uncomfortable to watch someone dissolve into tears or turn beet-red with rage. We feel helpless. Our uncomfortableness prompts us to make comments like "Calm down!" or "Snap out of it!" or "Quit overreacting!" What we really are saying is a coded command: "Control your emotions; put the lid on your feelings." That's what we all tell each other—and ourselves. "Hold it all in," we say. "Don't let anything spill out. Control yourself."

What good does that do? Actually, it doesn't do *any* good. Ignoring or avoiding painful emotions won't make them go away. The fact is that emotions will always come out. One way or another, strong feelings will boil to the surface—usually when you least expect them.

You can ignore, deny, or hold in your emotions only so long and then—*Blam!*—they explode. Often without warning.

Mandy liked Tom more than any boy she had ever met. She thought about him nearly every minute of the day. Whenever she sat across from him in study hall, her heart nearly stopped.

One day he asked her out, and numb with ecstasy, she

accepted. All that day she thought about him and fantasized about what a wonderful date they would have.

Unfortunately, Tom never showed up. Seven o'clock came and went. At nine, Mandy, sorely disappointed, gave up and went out for a Coke with some friends. They walked into the Dairy Queen and there sat Tom with a girl from another school.

Mandy was crushed.

At school the next day, Mandy acted as if nothing had happened. At home she seemed her usual self, though a little quieter than usual. But her mother finally noticed that something was wrong. "Mandy, you've been moping around a lot lately, picking at your food, and griping at your sister," she said. "You used to rush off to school in the morning and you've been late twice this week. What's the matter?"

Mandy let her have it with both barrels. "You're always prying into my life!" she screamed. "Why don't you just mind your own business? I don't go around snooping after you! Why can't people leave me alone?" She stormed out of the house and hopped in the car despite her mother's protests. She backed out of the driveway in such a hurry that she ran over her little brother's bike and scraped the paint on the car's rear fender.

THE TRUTH ABOUT FEELINGS

It's easy to see what happened to Mandy. She held in her anger and disappointment, letting them simmer beneath the surface until the pressure became so great that she blew up. Most of us probably would say that she let her negative emotions get the best of her, or that she "gave in" to bad feelings.

The truth is that our feelings are neither good nor bad. Feelings are just feelings. They are neutral. How you react to your feelings, however, is *not* neutral. Your responses can be either positive or negative. This is an important point to remember: The way you handle powerful feelings can be good or bad, but the emotions themselves are neutral.

When we label a strong emotion as either "good" or "bad," we imply that some feelings are healthy, normal, and acceptable, while others are unhealthy, abnormal, and definitely not acceptable.

Therefore, having a "bad" feeling makes us somehow unhealthy or abnormal.

But Mandy wasn't abnormal because she felt disappointment and anger when Tom ditched out on their date. She felt the way she felt; her feelings were simply her body's spontaneous response to her powerful thought, *I've been stood up!* Feelings are largely physical reactions to powerful thoughts.

Your mind and body are interconnected in subtle ways. The mind thinks and the body reacts to the thought. An emotion, then, is how your body "interprets" a thought. You simply cannot choose how you feel any more than you can choose not to get wet when you jump into the water. You think a thought and your body reacts. It's that simple.

When you feel fearful, for example, it's because you *think* you are being threatened. Feeling depressed is a sign that you think you have lost something. Anger is your body's way of reacting to the thought that an injustice has been done to you.

Since emotions are merely physical sensations associated with thoughts, and the thoughts are not always wrong, there is no way the emotions themselves can be considered good or bad.

MANAGING PAINFUL FEELINGS

Emotions may be neutral, but what you do with them—or what you let them do to you—can certainly be labeled good or bad, constructive or destructive, wholesome or unhealthy.

For example, if Jim stomps onto the court and punches out the ref for benching him, he obviously has chosen a destructive way of handling his anger. If Wendy vows to never again return to school, she has handled rejection badly. If Rick continues feeding his hurt and distrust, he has given in to unhealthy behavior.

Handling painful emotions in a healthy, positive way isn't easy. It's extremely difficult to channel anger or to express hurt or jealousy constructively. Painful feelings seem to drop out of the sky like meteorites. They hit you on the head, hurt like fury, and leave you wounded and bewildered. When you are forced to cope with your feelings the best way you can, it is easy to feel trapped by what seems beyond your control.

Still, you can learn to manage your emotions. It is possible for you to work through your powerful feelings and to allow something good to come from the pain. Following the four steps listed below can help you cope with your feelings and weather your emotional storms in good shape.

1. *Identify your feelings.* When something really painful happens, it isn't unusual for all kinds of feelings to meld together. So many emotions may sweep through you that it is difficult to know exactly *what* you're feeling.

The first step in managing your feelings is to identify what it is you are feeling. If you cannot pinpoint the emotion, see the feelings sampler on page 53. Sometimes just seeing the words in this list can help you figure out what you're feeling. However, it may not always be quite that easy.

Another way to identify your emotions is to check your body for clues. Are your muscles tense? Are you grinding your teeth or clenching your fists? Are you crying? Is your heart pounding? Are you tired or sleepy? Is it difficult to concentrate on what you're doing? Remember, your mind and body are interconnected—what goes on in one is mirrored in the other.

Your physical sensations can be traced to emotions in fairly predictable ways. If your stomach is tight, you may be anxious about something. If you are tired and lethargic, you may be depressed. If your jaws hurt from clenching your teeth, you may be very angry.

Another emotion identifier is to get out a piece of paper and a pen and write down everything you are feeling. You might start with unrelated words and sentences, or you might write down your thoughts as though you were writing a letter to an understanding friend or to God. Don't worry about anyone really reading what you've written—no one will. Just write your feelings out and see what happens. When you've finished, look for key emotion words like *depressed, restless, frustrated, worried,* etc.

Yet another method is to go someplace where you can be completely alone and give a speech expressing your point of view to an imaginary listener. You don't have to be fair. Don't hold back or worry about hurting anyone's feelings—just get it out. Tell what happened, who you blame. You can even blame God if you want.

Point your finger at the person who wronged you; be specific. Notice the feeling words that come out in your speech.

Here's one last technique to try. Complete the sentence, "The last time I felt like this was . . ." The past often holds clues to the present. You may be experiencing feelings of loneliness if you completed the sentence like this: "The last time I felt like this was when Mom and Dad left me at Grandma's for a week. I thought they had abandoned me."

Most important, when trying to understand your feelings forget how you *should* feel and focus on how you *do* feel. Feelings are often confusing because a person doesn't label them accurately. If someone close to you has died, for example, you may think you should feel sad, when in reality you feel angry or relieved. After working very hard to get something you wanted, you may think you should feel happy, while what you really feel is disappointment or ambivalence. It's no good to tell yourself you should feel one way when you really feel another. Forget how you think you ought to feel or how someone else might feel. Ask yourself, *What am I* really *feeling?*

2. *Express your feelings.* It may not be easy for you to express your feelings. You may encounter resistance from other people when you let your feelings show. Since most people don't know how to express their feelings appropriately, society often restrains emotional expression. That's why a coach will say, "Cool off!" or a parent will say, "Snap out of it!"

The answer to this is to learn how to express your emotions appropriately—at the right time, in the right place, and in the right way. There are two rules to keep in mind that will help you avoid doing anything that will make a situation worse than it already is: (1) Do not hurt living things, either people or animals. Don't punch a friend or kick the dog; and (2) Do not destroy property. This means anything of value to yourself or another person. Fight the urge to slash the speech teacher's tires, egg your neighbor's house, or heave your mother's hand-cut crystal bowl into the fireplace. Throwing a rock through a picture window is out, but lambasting a punching bag is in.

A subrule to both of the above rules is: *Never drive when you are upset.* It is likely that you will hurt someone or damage property if you drive when you are experiencing intense feelings. The results can be drastic and tragic.

On the more positive side, see pages 55–56 for a list of appropriate ways to express your emotions.

3. *Analyze your feelings.* Once you've identified and expressed your feelings, you will want to consider what they mean and try to match what you are feeling with what you are thinking. Someone who has been stood up for a date will probably feel angry and disappointed, but she needs to understand why. Is it because the date itself was so important or is it because she now feels rejected and without self-confidence?

Emotions can be elusive, giving few clues as to what is really going on in your mind. That's when you need to play detective and do a little investigating. Recall what happened—as painful as that might be—and reflect on what the event meant to you. Work at remembering the situation; often the thoughts were there, along with the emotions.

In discovering the thought behind the feelings, you might realize that the thought is based on wrong information. For example, you might feel anxious because you think that you are going to fail a chemistry exam. But you know that you have studied, that you have kept up with class assignments, and are well-prepared. You do not have a valid reason for your fear. When you realize this and your thoughts change from apprehension to confidence, your anxiety will dissipate.

On the other hand, if what you think is fact—you *were* treated unfairly by the ref, or you *did* embarrass yourself when you failed to get a part in the play—then you have an opportunity to deal with the truth, to change the situation or yourself, or to accept the situation. If you think you got a raw deal and that's what's making you angry, then try finding out how it happened and see if there's anything you can do to change things. If you think you have lost something of value and that's what's making you depressed, then take steps to regain or replace what you've lost.

4. *React appropriately to your feelings.* Our tendency is to react negatively to painful situations, whether the reaction is kicking the cat or saying something that we will later regret. It is possible to become slaves to our feelings.

Powerful emotions will take up as much time and energy as you allow them to. If you let them, they will control you, toss you to and fro, deprive you of the upper hand. Your emotions can take over your life.

To control negative reactions is to curb inappropriate expressions and to learn appropriate ones. When painful feelings threaten to get out of control, try one of the following techniques:

■ A good round of intense physical exercise can work wonders—it loosens up tense muscles, stimulates circulation, and feeds oxygen-enriched blood to the brain, which helps clear up fuzzy thinking. If you can make your body feel better, you'll start feeling better emotionally, too.

Exercise also releases pent-up energy and helps you relax more easily. Relaxation, especially after a good workout, promotes feelings of pleasure and contentment. It's hard to feel depressed or anxious or angry when your muscles are relaxed; they refuse to hold tension. If your body is relaxed, your mind will relax, too.

■ People say laughter is the best medicine. It's true. If you can still laugh, in spite of what you're feeling, you will be much closer to getting back to normal. This doesn't mean that you should try to laugh away your problems—just put your feelings in perspective: "I feel bad, but these bad feelings aren't going to dominate me. I still have my sense of humor. I can keep things in perspective."

Laughter has proven to have beneficial physical and psychological effects. It's a curative. Read a joke book, watch an old sitcom—anything that will help you laugh.

■ You don't have to deal with your emotions nonstop. Sometimes you may need to check out for a while, to take a break from the feelings that have been causing you pain. This doesn't mean that you are running away from reality or burying your emotions and denying them. You're just putting them aside for a time.

■ A change of scenery—jogging downtown, walking in the park, biking in the country—can help divert your attention. Reading a good book, spending time in prayer and meditation or Bible study, or visiting a friend will give your mind and emotions a break. Afterwards, you will be stronger and better able to deal with your problems.

■ Allow yourself opportunities to regroup and recharge your batteries. Say to yourself, "This, too, shall pass." You've heard that before, but it's more than just a trite phrase. Even the deepest pains—the death of a loved one, a horrible injury, the ruination of a lifetime dream—eventually pass. Though it seems impossible, you *will* put your life back together. You *will* survive. You *will* go on.

Hold on to the hope that what you are going through will eventually be resolved—it will help you keep your feelings and pain in perspective. Right now there may not seem to be a way out, but you won't have to live with the intensity of the pain forever.

THE FEELINGS PARADOX

Expressing feelings, controlling them, avoiding them in order to deal with them better, experiencing them so that they will pass more quickly—all of this plays a part in the proper handling of painful emotions. That's the paradox of feelings. At times you need to express them, at other times you need to control them, and then there are times you need to put them off for a while in order to gain a better perspective on them. Yet you can't avoid or deny painful feelings forever without serious consequences.

By identifying, expressing, analyzing, and controlling your painful emotions, you will emerge healthier, stronger, and with fewer scars.

YOUR TURN

What Are You Feeling?

Too many of us recognize only a few of our feelings—emotions such as anger, sadness, or happiness. If we're going to accurately identify our emotions, which is the first step in successfully dealing with them, we've got to be more specific. Next time you're not sure exactly what you're feeling, refer to the following list of possibilities.

(In fact, why not try it out right now. Think of one situation in the last week when something was going on with your emotions. Then go through this list and put a check next to the words that describe what you felt.)

POSSIBLE FEELINGS

__ ABANDONED	__ CHALLENGED	__ DUMB
__ ABUSED	__ COMPETITIVE	__ ELATED
__ AFRAID	__ CONCERNED	__ ENRAGED
__ AGGRAVATED	__ CONFUSED	__ ENVIED
__ ALIENATED	__ DEFENSIVE	__ ENVIOUS
__ AMBIVALENT	__ DELIGHTED	__ ERRATIC
__ AMUSED	__ DEPRESSED	__ EXCLUDED
__ ANGRY	__ DEPRIVED	__ EXPLOITED
__ ANTAGONISTIC	__ DESPERATE	__ FANTASTIC
__ ANXIOUS	__ DISAPPOINTED	__ FEARFUL
__ APATHETIC	__ DISILLUSIONED	__ FOOLISH
__ APPRECIATIVE	__ DISSATISFIED	__ FRIENDLY
__ APPREHENSIVE	__ DISTRACTED	__ FRUITY
__ BELITTLED	__ DISTRUSTING	__ FRUSTRATED
__ BITTER	__ DOOMED	__ GENEROUS
__ BORED	__ DOUBTFUL	__ GLOOMY

- GOOD-HUMORED
- GREEDY
- GRIEVED
- GUILTY
- HEROIC
- HONORED
- HOPELESS
- HOSTILE
- HURT
- HYSTERICAL
- IMMATURE
- IMPORTANT
- IMPULSIVE
- INADEQUATE
- INCLUDED
- INCOMPETENT
- INEFFICIENT
- INHIBITED
- INSECURE
- IRRATIONAL
- IRRITABLE
- ISOLATED
- JEALOUS
- JINXED
- JUBILANT
- JUMPY

- LETHARGIC
- LONELY
- LOST
- LOVED
- MALADJUSTED
- MATURE
- MELANCHOLY
- MISJUDGED
- MISUNDERSTOOD
- MOODY
- NEUROTIC
- NOBLE
- NUMBED
- PARANOID
- PERSECUTED
- POPULAR
- PREOCCUPIED
- PRESSURED
- PRIVILEGED
- REBELLIOUS
- REGRETFUL
- REJECTED
- REMORSEFUL
- REPULSED
- RESPECTED
- RESPONSIBLE

- RESTLESS
- REVENGEFUL
- SAD
- SCATTERED
- SHY
- SUPPORTED
- SURPRISED
- SUSPICIOUS
- TENSE
- TRIUMPHANT
- UNCOORDINATED
- UNDERSTOOD
- UNHAPPY
- UNMOTIVATED
- UNPRODUCTIVE
- UNREASONABLE
- UNSOCIABLE
- UNSTABLE
- UPSET
- USEFUL
- VALUED
- VICTIMIZED
- VULNERABLE
- WELCOME
- WITHDRAWN
- WORRIED

Express Your Feelings Positively!

Here are a few effective yet harmless ways you can express anger or other "negative" emotions when, for whatever reason, you're not able to talk about your feelings with the person(s) involved. These suggestions are not intended to be substitutes for talking. Whenever possible, you should attempt to confront the other person directly, with the goal of mutual understanding. But if the other person isn't around, or you feel like punching somebody, try one or more of the following suggestions instead. They will help you face your feelings without having to act them out in destructive ways.

After reading the list, you'll probably come up with other ideas of your own.

- Go for a long, hard bike ride.
- Lift weights in the school gym.
- Go someplace where you won't be heard and scream at the top of your lungs.
- Tell all your feelings to your dog or cat.
- Write a letter to the person(s) who triggered the feelings, expressing exactly how you feel, no holds barred. Don't worry about being tactful; just say how it all feels from your perspective. (However, do *not* send the letter!)
- Call a "hot line" and tell a sympathetic stranger how you feel.
- Go to a driving range and hit a bucket of golf balls as hard and as far as you possibly can.

- Play handball or racquetball by yourself; imagine the ball is whatever or whoever caused you the pain.
- Hit a tennis ball against a practice wall or shoot baskets.
- Jump on a trampoline.
- Cry.
- Jog or do wind sprints.
- Write a poem or compose a song about how you feel.
- Play and sing along with some records that express your feelings.
- Punch a pillow or punching bag until you have worked through all of your emotions.
- Do aerobic exercises to music.
- Draw a picture or sketch of how you feel.
- Talk into a tape recorder; dump everything onto the tape and then listen carefully to yourself.
- Take a long walk.
- Pray—tell God everything; don't hold back, just let him hear it all.

Faith and feelings. There is no "Christian" way to avoid powerful and painful feelings. Even though many people assume that "real Christians" never get angry or depressed or experience anything but happiness and bliss all their days, we all know the truth: Christians, too, suffer painful feelings.

Unfortunately, many Christians add an additional weight to their already painful feelings: the weight of guilt. They believe that if they were better Christians life would be all sunshine and roses. If they were better Christians, they'd never feel bad at all.

But your feelings are as much a part of you as the color of your hair and the size of your feet. Just as you don't choose to have brown or blue eyes, neither do you choose grief, depression, humiliation, or whatever. These emotions spring up from inside you because you are human. So, in that sense, your emotions are God-given. They are as individual as your fingerprints.

The difference is that while you can't do anything about your fingerprints, you *can* do something about the way you deal with your emotions. When they surface, you do have choices. You can ignore them, deny them, lock them up tight, wallow in them, give in to them, let them take over . . . or you can accept them as a part of who you are and use them to help you understand yourself better and to make you a stronger person.

Jesus got angry, he wept, he suffered anxiety (once to the point of sweating blood). Yet he did not allow his painful emotions to rule him, nor did he try to hide them. He accepted them, but he expressed and dealt with them in appropriate ways. You can do the same. And as you do so, you will come closer to discovering the unique personality God meant you to have.

Your One-and-Only Personality

Steve Lawhead

When I first became a Christian I kept a close eye on the people around me. I watched the older people to see how I, as a Christian, would look and act. What kind of personality should I have? I wanted to be sure I got it right.

I saw right away that being a Christian was pretty serious business—in church you didn't smile or talk. Sunday school was worse—an hour of reading and lecture. We had to be quiet in class, too, because anyone who told a joke or made a funny remark would be punished by being called upon to close the meeting with a prayer.

I lived in fear of meetings with other Christians because I wasn't very good at praying out loud in front of people. I was doubly fearful because my active sense of humor made me a prime candidate for that odd punishment.

It was hard to be as stoic as everyone seemed to expect me to be. Church became a chore—a stifling, numbing ordeal to be endured week after week. The people I looked to for guidance seemed as bored with the whole thing as I was.

Being a Christian meant a stern formality.

Stiff.

Unimaginative.

Unnatural.

I was readily familiar with the concept of "giving up" something to follow Christ—giving up smoking, or drinking, or using four-letter words. But I began feeling that I'd have to give up my personality. I wasn't so sure that being a Christian was worth it.

Luckily, something happened to rescue me: I grew up. I began to see that my ideas of Christianity were much too small. Christ did not want to stifle my personality any more than I did. I didn't have to be a sad-eyed monk with the personality of a dead mackerel. God wanted me to be very much *me*—sense of humor and all.

After I came to that realization (and it took a few years), I saw Jesus in a new way. He was not primarily a "man of sorrows," but a man of joy. A joy that is expressed in brilliant, living technicolor—instead of unvarying shades of gray. He spoke out most harshly against those who made religion a tiresome burden. The more I found out about this Jesus, the more I saw him as one with an unquenchable enthusiasm, whose smile was never far from his lips.

Sadly, the people around me in my early years as a Christian didn't show me that side of God. I wish I'd known from the beginning that my sense of humor was safe with God. (After all, he designed the kangaroo and the platypus.) A God who delights in all the richness and complexity of life that he has created isn't about to stop me from enjoying it with him.

YOUR TURN

Name That Personality

Remember "Louie" in chapter one? She tried to adopt the personalities of people she admired. Ultimately it backfired on her when she lost touch with who she really was. She had to go back to being honest with herself and learn to like who she was.

So try it. Put an "X" where you think you belong on the following scales.

Remember, *there is no right or wrong way to be.* As Steve Lawhead learned, God is very pleased when you are what he created you to be—with your own vivid, unique personality.

PERSONALITY SCALE

Outgoing	Reserved
Emotional	Thoughtful
Talkative	Quiet
Like to try new things	Stick with tried-and-true
Would rather compete	Would rather cooperate
Happy-go-lucky	Serious
Imaginative	Practical
Prefer groups	Prefer being alone
Laid-back	Self-disciplined
Like to "go with the flow"	Like to plan
Trusting	Cautious

WORDS OTHERS USE TO DESCRIBE MY PERSONALITY
(GO AHEAD, ASK THEM.)

Mom	Dad	Brother	Sister

Best friend	Pastor	Teacher	Other

Using Affirmations to Gain Self-Acceptance

If you have found from this and earlier journal exercises that you have a poor self-image—that you basically don't like yourself much—try the following technique. It's called *affirmation*.

Affirmation is based on a simple idea: You can hold only one thought in your head at a time. When you consistently replace negative thoughts with positive thoughts, the positive thoughts have the power to cancel out the negative. The Bible says, "As [a man] thinks in his heart, so is he" (Prov. 23:7 NKJV). Positive thoughts are affirmations, and affirmations are a powerful way to grow toward self-acceptance.

There are a couple of different ways to use affirmations. One is to look at yourself in a mirror, maintain eye contact, and say *out loud*, "[Your name], I love you and accept you just the way you are," or "[Your name], God loves you and accepts you just as you are and so do I." It is very helpful to repeat such affirmations when you need them—when you or someone else puts you down.

Other possible affirmations are: "God loves me and uses me in spite of my shortcomings," "I like myself always and in all ways," "I never have to apologize for being me."

An even more effective way to use affirmations is to write them out in your journal. You can pick an affirmation that you don't yet believe but that you would like to believe. Write it out twenty times every time you write in your journal, and after each affirmation write the first response that comes to your mind. For example:

"I, Diane, would not trade me for anyone."

Are you kidding? I would much rather be Carol, she's so poised and attractive.

"I, Diane, would not trade me for anyone."

If only I weren't so klutzy.

"I, Diane, would not trade me for anyone."

But I'm too short.

"I, Diane, would not trade me for anyone."

I'm not popular with guys.

"I, Diane, would not trade me for anyone."

I guess sometimes I like being me.

"I, Diane, would not trade me for anyone."

I guess I do have some good points.

"I, Diane, would not trade me for anyone."

But some of the kids at school don't like me.

"I, Diane, would not trade me for anyone."

I just wish my brothers wouldn't bug me so much about certain things.

"I, Diane, would not trade me for anyone."

I guess I'll never be great, but I can probably be good enough.

"I, Diane, would not trade me for anyone."

Am I good enough for God?

"I, Diane, would not trade me for anyone."

My friends seem to like me the way I am.

"I, Diane, would not trade me for anyone."

But my parents are always telling me I'm too moody. If only I could be less moody.

"I, Diane, would not trade me for anyone."

Maybe it doesn't really matter that I get moody sometimes.

"I, Diane, would not trade me for anyone."

Would I really want to be Carol? I heard her parents just got divorced.

"I, Diane, would not trade me for anyone."

Maybe my shortcomings aren't any worse than anyone else's.

"I, Diane, would not trade me for anyone."

I'm not perfect, but who is?

"I, Diane, would not trade me for anyone."

No matter what anyone else thinks of me, the Bible says God accepts me.

"I, Diane, would not trade me for anyone."

Those people who shut me out hardly even know me.

"I, Diane, would not trade me for anyone."

Why should I be as hard on me as those people are? Who says they're more right than I am about me?

"I, Diane, would not trade me for anyone."

I guess it is good to be me.

If you practice this several times a day in your journal, within a few weeks the positive thoughts will gradually replace the negative thoughts. As you replace the old, negative labels with positive truths about who you are and what you want to become, you smash any distorting inner mirrors that may be affecting your self-image.

Your Unique Creativity

Jim Long

There's nothing like a twenty-minute drum solo to relieve pent-up emotions—for the drummer, especially. There are crescendos of thundering power and calm valleys of controlled rhythm. It is not at all surprising to me that the Bible talks about praising God with drums and cymbals. A drum solo can be a handy reflection of the power of God—or even, for that matter, of his sensitivity.

Unfortunately, not all Christians share my affectionate assessment of the worth of Mylar skins and glistening brass. In fact, when I became a Christian, my drums posed a conflict for me. I was made to feel my involvement in rock music was evil.

It wasn't just the words of the rock songs that created problems for me. (I still consider the rock music world a vast moral wasteland—particularly lyrically.) My music hassles went beyond the lyrics to the music itself. I was constantly getting subtle and sometimes not-so-subtle impressions from other Christians: *Music with a beat or a strong driving rhythm is sinful, pagan, barbaric.*

That was sure death to a drummer. I might as well have broken the sticks. As a new believer, the approval of older Christian leaders was more important to me than the drums I enjoyed, so I sold out. I quit the neighborhood rock group, passed up an offer from a friend's band (they already had recording contract offers), and instead hung out my free-lance-drumming shingle. But I knew it was all over.

I did a few free-lance jobs with, oddly enough, some middle-aged men who played Lawrence Welk-style music ... but that didn't last either.

Then came the big Jesus movement, which would have been a perfect outlet for all this creative energy. Unfortunately, the movement was just getting started and was regarded with suspicion by older Christians who cautioned me against it. Even though I did not understand why it was so wrong, I accepted the leadership of these older Christians—after all, I was new to this Christianity thing—and the final existing outlet for my drums was laid to rest. (At the time there wasn't much call for drum solos as church offertories.)

Since then, I often have wondered, *Why wasn't I encouraged to develop and use my creative interests?* It wasn't just my interest in music. I also loved art and dabbled in it a great deal over the years. It was never important enough to develop a high degree of artistic skillfulness (though the church occasionally needed a poster to hang in the furnace room promoting the youth group's car wash).

Strangely, I never had to look for Christians who would encourage me to *study*—they came out of the woodwork of the pews. "Study the Word," they would say. "Show yourself approved." Or they would intone, "Get good grades for God." All of that is fine, but no one prodded my interest in art or nudged me toward excellence in my creativity.

Then there was my high school creative writing teacher who liked one of my stories so much that she didn't believe I wrote it. That promoted mixed emotions, but I didn't receive even "mixed encouragement" from Christians to develop my writing. Always there were other things that were considered more important: meetings to attend, talks to listen to, pamphlets to read. And I wondered: *Why haven't I been encouraged to develop and use my creative interests?*

In some ways I was a model conversion story. After becoming a Christian during my senior year of high school, my interests, drives, attitudes, and behavior changed radically. I turned my room into a makeshift monastery and spent all my extra coins not on records, but on religious books. I devoured them to the point of indigestion.

"I will be a minister," I told myself, "or a Bible college or seminary prof—*possibly* a missionary." The older Christians were proud of the transformed kid. I went to a Christian liberal arts college and from there to seminary. Then, suddenly, as a student in a midwestern seminary, that old creative urge surfaced again. I saw in a fresh way the need for Christians to be involved in the arts, to use their creativity and communication skills to reflect the beauty and creativity of God, and to make large artistic dents for God in people's defensive shells.

This new awareness did not come through my seminary studies as I thumbed dog-eared Hebrew vocabulary cards. It came through key friendships with Christians who were involved in the arts, using their creativity and communication skills for God. And I wondered again: *Why wasn't I encouraged to develop and use my creative interests?*

I don't mean to bad-mouth Bible college, seminary, Christian leaders, or Bible study. I needed a good grounding in the Bible. But the fact that I had such varied creative interests should have told me something. God does not want Bible wizards who have computer-like recall of Scripture verses but lack love for beauty and the artistic expression of our God-given creative talents.

I wish I'd known sooner that I didn't have to bushwhack my creativity and bury my talents to be a Christian. I am accountable for my creativity; I am responsible for how I use my talents. God is interested in my creative flair. He loves to work through the things that bring me joy—even the drums.

YOUR TURN

Jim Long reminds us that each of us is unique in the things we care about. What turns *you* on?

Here is a list of examples to get your thoughts churning: music (singing, listening, playing the drums or piano or flute); writing (stories, poetry, essays); math (geometry, algebra, trigonometry); science (biology, genetics, physics); photography; hang gliding; skiing; sports (watching, playing, or both); helping people (old, young, your peers—and how you like to help them); fixing things; teaching; learning new things (sewing, hiking, dancing, spelunking, drawing, painting, sculpting); making furniture; cooking.

Things I've Tried That Interest Me:

_____

_____

Things I'd *Like* to Try:

_____

_____

Does any important person(s) disapprove? Who? Of which interests? Why?

_____

_____

Your Unique Dreams

Dan Robbins

I'm not an expert on dreams. I've never had my brain waves recorded and analyzed. I've never even discussed my memories of childhood with a psychiatrist. I just dream.

I'm not talking about those surrealistic mind-movies that play on the back of my eyelids when I sleep. And I'm not referring to spiritual visions where I hear voices directing my life choices. As a fairly normal, young, somewhat idealistic, single, part-time graduate student, I do a lot of dreaming. In the quiet cracks of time between busy moments, I've discovered a lot of time to think about the future, to hope for better times, and to dream. About everything. And anything. I highly recommend it.

I've asked a number of other people, "Do you dream?" Most people seem reluctant to discuss the particulars of their dreams. When I queried one friend about his dreams, he smiled warily and responded, "Why do you want to know? Are you going to write this down somewhere?" Other friends have said, "I have this dream, but I've never told anyone about it." Sometimes our dreams are too close, too personal. They tell more of who we are than we may want to reveal.

In high school I dreamed of having a good best friend. I had grown up reading *Hardy Boys* stories and the idea of a close, trusted friend was appealing. We could do things together, anything: visit exotic places, solve or even create mysteries, develop elaborate money-making projects, invent and mess up, or just bum around when life got to be dull.

I spent a lot of time bumming around by myself, mainly because I never told anyone about my dream. Nor did I ever try to make it come true by being a really good friend to anyone else.

Over time, as I've worked up the courage to share my dreams with others, I've made the exciting discovery that a lot of other people have dreams, too. I've come to suspect that almost everyone has a growing, reaching, struggling collection of goals—aspirations so personal they are afraid to tell anyone else for fear they will be thought immodest, impractical, or even silly.

I've also come to understand that our dreams will never be more than wasted imagination unless we do something with them. And that truly would be a waste, because dreams, properly used, can motivate us to change and shape our futures.

DANGERS IN DREAMWORLD

Unfortunately, not all dreams are healthy. I've known some people who were so caught up in their dreams they seemed to forget present-day reality.

Stan and John are big dreamers, but their dreams are incorporated into the fantasy game *Dungeons and Dragons*. In reality, Stan and John both have higher goals and aspirations for the future—goals for better education, good jobs, and closer relationships with friends. Yet they spend a lot of time in their game, creating some new fantasy adventure, which leaves little time for their other dreams and goals.

I see danger signals in this type of dreaming. I, too, have my fantasies—dreams that often involve sex or special relationships, expensive living, fame or fortune. Not unlike sleeping dreams, these fantasies are absurd mutations of reality and they often leave me feeling confused, guilty, frustrated. Dreams for pleasure may be OK in small doses, but in the long run they just waste time. Good dreams have to be more than mere fantasy.

BUT DO DREAM ON

How do you dream realistically *and* effectively? Realistic dreaming, geared toward healthy goals and a realistic future, requires two important elements: relaxation and research.

Relaxation in dreaming is important. In college, my worst

brainstorming sessions were attempted while my roommate, Greg, was rocking out on my stereo. He would be sound asleep on the floor while vast decibels of Kansas were shaking plaster from the walls. He may have been able to unwind, but I couldn't. When I'm trying to figure the future, I need a quiet and relaxing environment. I can't think with a lot of noise or a hectic, busy schedule.

To balance relaxation, research also is important. Research sounds dull and serious—like something you have to do for a term paper. It doesn't have to be. It can be the first in a series of practical steps toward fulfilling a dream. My father, a magazine publisher, helped me work out my plan for becoming a writer. When I was right out of high school, I didn't have the slightest idea what I wanted to do for a career, or a major, or anything. (Graduating from high school will do that to you.) My father suggested, "Make a list of the things you like or want to do, whether in classes, activities, or whatever. Then come talk to me about it." I did and we both noted that there were certain trends toward particular interests, which could then be translated into a college major and ultimately a career.

In addition to my self-survey, my research also included investigating and discussing my dreams with others—trusted friends, teachers, parents. For me, this was the most difficult part of the dream process. But it is also the most necessary, because only by opening up this part of ourselves can we see how similar we are to others.

The anguish of our dreams diminishes as we share them. Friends can help us balance our emotions and idealism. Listening to older wisdom can help guide our judgments. Also, once we articulate our dreams it's easier to judge them by the light of God's guidance, which we can seek through prayer and Bible study.

By taking time to research and to talk my dreams out, I became convinced of what I wanted to do with my life. More important, I became convinced of what God wanted me to do.

Ultimately, dreams are what you make of them. Do something with yours. Share them, then listen. You may be surprised where they take you.

YOUR TURN

Daydreams

Who are you? You're not just a person sitting and reading this book at this moment. You're not just a recipe made up of feelings, personality characteristics, and interests. You're also a person who is *becoming* something more. You're moving in the direction of your dreams. To understand your uniqueness, you must know your dreams.

When I was younger, I used to dream about _____

_____

I dream best when _____

_____

Most of the time I dream about _____

_____

The one dream I would really like to see come true is _____

_____

Have you told anybody about your dreams? If not, why not?

_____

_____

MY DREAM:

_____

_____

_____

Here are some steps I can take to make my dream some true:

1. _____

2. _____

3. _____

4. _____

5. _____

6. _____

7. _____

I, _____, would like to begin the steps I've listed above by _____ (date) and achieve my dream by the time I am _____ years old.

_____
signature

Physical

Therefore, I urge you, brothers, in view of God's mercy, to offer your bodies as living sacrifices, holy and pleasing to God—this is your spiritual act of worship.

(Romans 12:1)

Measuring Up: I Used to Compare Myself to Jim Patterson

Richard McAfee

Whenever Jim Patterson passed me in the hallway at school, I noticed. Everyone noticed Jim Patterson, especially girls. His body was molded to perfection. When Jim was not playing football, he was lifting weights; when not lifting weights, he was training for the wrestling team. He seemed to have everything going for him. Passing Jim in the hallway always made me sad. The lines of his muscular torso moved gracefully.

I was overweight. People noticed me in the hallway, too, but rather than sighing breathlessly in admiration, they snickered at my bulges. Wearing braces on my teeth wasn't any help. Weight lifting bored me. I was too clumsy to play football, and too chicken to wrestle (I could just imagine some big brute rubbing my braces into the mat). With all those things going against me, I determined I would never look like Jim Patterson. I was right.

Barbara Clemson was my dream love. How could anyone be both a drum majorette and cheerleader in the same year? All the girls wished they were Barbara. I wished I was Barbara's. Unfortunately, Barbara was not a chubby-chaser. On the contrary, she liked Jim Patterson. She was more into brawn than brains. And brains were the only thing I could offer. I lost.

Why are football trophies displayed in a school's front-hallway showcase and debate trophies stored in the speech teacher's bottom drawer? I worked just as hard to win that debate trophy as Jim Patterson worked to win the league football trophy. Oh well, such is the life of an everyday scholar.

Graduation came. I received a scholarship to UCLA. To my horror and dismay, Jim Patterson also won a scholarship—athletic, of course—to none other than UCLA. Had cheerleading scholarships been available, we would have been a threesome. They weren't, so I don't know what happened to dreamy Barbara. Fall came, and Jim and I said good-bye to our high-school friends. I think he promised Barbara he would return to her—something about tying a yellow ribbon around the old oak tree. She may still be waiting.

Then, suddenly it seemed, my life began to change. In modern literature class we read Franz Kafka's *Metamorphosis.* You know—the story about the guy who went to bed and woke the next morning a bug. I experienced the same thing—except, thankfully, I went to bed as a bug and awoke a guy. My dentist, bless her heart, removed the tinsel from my teeth during the first-semester Thanksgiving holiday. (First time I had eaten Thanksgiving dinner in years that I didn't have to spend the afternoon with pick and axe, removing turkey and the trimmings from my metalware.) I could smile without blinding the world. Furthermore, my new self-image encouraged me to diet. I discovered that firsts could be just as satisfying as fourths and fifths. The pounds began to drop. I was still not Jim Patterson, but I was improving.

I discovered, too, that not every young woman who generated my romantic interest looked first at bodies and only second at brains. I don't know what happened to Jim Patterson—but you know, for the first time in my life it didn't really matter. I had a new person to try to measure up to—myself.

YOUR TURN

How you feel about your body is an important part of who you are. Learning to accept and, yes, even appreciate every part of your body is a tremendously liberating experience.

MY BODY

What I like about my body is

_____

_____

_____

What I *don't* like about my body is

_____

_____

_____

Can any of these change? What would it take?

_____

_____

_____

You and Your Body: the Bible's Perspective

It's important that we keep physical appearance in perspective. That's what Richard McAfee learned: Life is more than the shape of your body. You might read about his comparisons with Jim Patterson and conclude: Bodies aren't important. We should ignore them and concentrate on more significant aspects of life. But that would be going too far in the other direction.

Some Christians have tried to treat their bodies as unimportant. To them, the spiritual is what matters and the physical side of life is, if not downright sinful in itself, at least a temptation to sin. The physical body is a prison to be put up with until they die and escape and begin their true life in Christ as pure spirits.

But this is not what the Bible teaches. God looked at the physical world he had made—water, plants, animals, birds—and saw that everything was "good" (Gen. 1:25). Then he made human beings in his own image, created them male and female, complete with sexual urges, and looked at them and called them "very good" (Gen. 1:31).

But what about sin? Didn't that mar everything? In one sense it did, but not by turning everything that once was good into something bad. Rather, the good was bent out of its proper shape, like a nail that won't go in until you straighten it. That's the way we are. Our bodies were meant to be good—to glorify God—but we use them to gratify our selfish desires. We can abuse our bodies through drugs, overeating, lack of rest, and the like. Not only do our bodies tend to go in the wrong direction, but every aspect of our lives goes wrong. Our emotions can lead us to do wrong things, and so can our thoughts. Because of sin we are incapable of changing ourselves or even knowing God on our own; but he has provided a way for us to come to him through Jesus, who took the punishment for our sin so we could live different lives.

The value of the body was affirmed when God himself "became flesh and made his dwelling among us" (John 1:14). Jesus lived a physical, human life on this earth. After he rose from the dead, he still had a body that could be touched (John 20:27–29), that apparently even needed food because he cooked breakfast and ate it with his disciples (John 21:9–13). When he ascended into heaven, he ascended bodily (Acts 1:9).

The Bible teaches that our bodies are essential to who we are. Someday there will be a great event called "the resurrection of the dead" when Christians will be raised from the dead and given new bodies like Christ's resurrection body (1 Cor. 15:35–44) and live in a new land (Rev. 20:11–21). In the meantime, we are to treat our present bodies with care and respect: "Don't you know that you yourselves are God's temple and that God's Spirit lives in you? If anyone destroys God's temple, God will destroy him; for God's temple is sacred, and you are that temple" (1 Cor. 3:16–17); "Therefore, I urge you, brothers, in view of God's mercy, to offer your bodies as living sacrifices, holy and pleasing to God—this is your spiritual act of worship" (Rom. 12:1).

Not only our bodies, but all physical things were created good. Though these things can be used for evil, God's original intention was that we enjoy all that he made. He could have made all food taste like broccoli; he could have made a colorless, black-and-white world; he could have made creation odorless, or made all things smell like sweat; he could have made people sexless and found another way to keep the human race going. But he didn't. He created a wildly diverse physical world, declared it "good," presented it to us, and then said, "Enjoy."

Hair Was Only Half My Problem

John Hamelin

We're to enjoy our bodies and all things God has created, using them to serve Christ. But it's sometimes impossible to appreciate and enjoy our bodies when we find parts of them unacceptable. So consider that list of things you hate about your body, and see what insights about self-acceptance you can glean from the following story.

When I was in the third grade my family moved from Florida to southern California. Getting used to new people and surroundings would have been hard anyway—but within a year of our arrival my hair started falling out in patches. Be glad if you don't ever experience standing in front of your mirror yanking hunks of hair out of your head. I know that compared to what some go through—a crippling disease, for instance—losing your hair is a small thing. But in my life it was everything. I thought of very little else.

I ignored it at first, hoping it would be strictly temporary. I was ashamed and afraid to admit there was anything wrong. But when they took class pictures, there was no hiding the little blotches where scalp showed through. Eventually all my hair fell out.

My parents took me to a series of doctors. One of them, I remember, tried to treat me by giving me thirty-five to fifty shots in my head. But it didn't work, and eventually the problem was diagnosed as alopecia—a disease that is incurable, isn't contagious, and doesn't affect anything except your hair. But what it did to my hair was enough.

Kids of grade-school age are at their meanest, I think. I wonder if they ever thought about what they were doing to me? For years I got called "Baldy" or "Cue Ball." The tough guys would make fun of me and pick on me. Others were just curious or teased me.

My reactions weren't very good. I became extremely self-conscious. I would take my frustrations out on kids who were younger or had greater problems than I did. One kid had a harelip, and another was extremely weak and frail. In my anger, I'd mimic and make fun of them, just as others did to me.

Before I started the seventh grade, I got a hairpiece. It was expensive, but for the first time in two years I looked almost normal. I remember putting it on and walking down to the bus for the first day of school, feeling really scared. I wondered if some of the kids who knew me would notice that I wore a wig. Would someone try to pull it off? What would girls think of me? I went through the day half-terrified, but nothing happened.

The kids who knew me were amazed at the transformation. From that day on things started getting better. Occasionally there would be insults, but not very often. People began to accept me more for who I was, and things improved a lot on the outside.

But real damage had been done inside me: I was terribly insecure. People would notice I was wearing a hairpiece, and naturally they'd be curious. I would feel them looking, trying to figure it out. I was terrified of having it slip at school so I'd have to adjust it. I didn't want strangers to see me without it, even for a second. I wouldn't participate in P.E. most of the time because if I sweat it would slip. A lot of times I used it as a crutch, getting out of sports and then sitting alone and feeling sorry for myself. My parents tried to help, always reminding me that people would eventually take me for what I was. But others wouldn't really be able to accept me until I accepted myself. And I hadn't done that.

By the time I was a sophomore in high school I'd become very offensive. If someone asked me an innocent question about why I wore a wig, I would jump down his throat. With no self-confidence, I couldn't fit into any group. I'd end up wandering from one to another, acting like a loudmouth. I wanted to have friends, but I really didn't know how to relate to people. I just made them uncomfortable.

I did have some friends, particularly in the neighborhood, with whom I could be more relaxed. When I was with those friends after school, I would even take off the wig (it's not the most comfortable thing to wear). I was learning, slowly, to accept myself and cope with people. In the winter of that sophomore year I started going to Campus Life, and that began making a big difference in my life.

I probably would never have gone if the group hadn't met at a girl's house across the street from where I lived. It had rained most of the day, so only fourteen people were there. That helped make it a warm and friendly atmosphere. It was a game night— there was not so much serious discussion as the meetings usually have, but lots of games. Everybody seemed to be willing to make a fool of himself.

I got involved and really had a good time. There hadn't been many times when I could enjoy myself without feeling self-conscious. I knew after that first meeting that I wanted to go back.

It wasn't just the fun—it was an atmosphere of acceptance. People in the club seemed more willing to take me for what I was. They still had questions, but it was easier to answer them. They didn't crack jokes to draw attention to my baldness. As I got involved with these people I began to relax.

At Easter vacation I got talked into going to an all-guy camp on Catalina Island. Actually, I wanted to go until I got on the boat and its pitching and rolling for the several-hour trip out to the island made me sick. People tried to comfort me, and I appreciated it, but I felt very much out of it. That night I was mostly over being sick, but I got a worse shock. The staff briefed us on our schedule for the week. They explained what Bible study was, and it hit me that this wasn't exactly like Boy Scout camp. They were serious about Christianity. But what upset me the most was when they said we'd be doing some waterskiing in the morning.

I'd never water-skied before; you can't water-ski with a wig. The thought of going out there bald terrified me. We were staying in big tents, and that evening I ran into John Selph, my Campus

Life club director. He'd shown a lot of patience with me, and had taken a special interest in me. I respected him. Our conversation was short—he asked me if I was going to do it, I said I didn't know, and he let me know in a kidding way that it was really an important step he'd like to see me take.

That night I lay awake while everyone else was sleeping and snoring, and wondered what I was doing at that camp. How did I get myself into things like this? But in the morning I knew I had to do it. I stripped off the wig and walked outside to join the others. Nobody hassled me. I felt real acceptance. And to top it off, I ended up waterskiing pretty well. That may sound like a small thing to you, but little steps like that have made a lot of difference for me. They've been made possible by the concerned, accepting environment I have found among Christians. I'm a Christian now, too—I made that crucial choice the summer after the Catalina Island camp.

In the following years, I became able to make a joke of my baldness, to laugh with people instead of cowering. Each little step has taken courage, courage I found coming from others' support and from Christ himself living in me.

I look back and wonder how I must have seemed to other people. I had two problems. First, I had a scalp disease that was somewhat unusual—perhaps unattractive—and second, I acted distant and made myself hard to like. The casual observer might never have realized there was a link between the two—he probably would have figured I was just a strange person who ought to be avoided.

But the two *were* linked together. I couldn't change my scalp, but I needed encouragement and acceptance to change my way of acting. That *could* change. Friends appreciating me—even when I didn't deserve appreciation in some ways—made it possible for me to have the courage I needed. They made me able to accept myself.

Alopecia is a rare disease, but self-hatred isn't. What helped me might work for a lot of other slightly strange-acting people who badly need acceptance.

YOUR TURN

Loving all of you

OK, now it's time to work on accepting—and even liking—those things you listed under "Things I Can't Change." Here are some suggestions. They are not easy to do, so you might try the one that seems easiest to you first, and go on to another after that. The more you can do, the more you will grow in accepting your body—and you'll be amazed at the freedom that brings.

1. *Open up to a trusted friend.* Find someone with whom you feel comfortable, someone who doesn't threaten you. You'll find it a surprising relief to confide to that person all your hidden misgivings about your appearance. Besides that, you might even get some positive feedback about parts of yourself that seem unattractive to you. And your friend probably has things about himself that are unacceptable to him, but that you don't mind at all. Opening up will help you put your feelings about your body into perspective.

Let me share a personal example. There are a couple of things I don't like about my body. My nose, for example, is long and rather pointed. In fact, once a little boy in the laundromat asked his mother, "Mommy, does that lady over there lie a lot?" His mother glanced over at me and, looking puzzled, said, "What do you mean?"

"Well," replied the little kid as if the answer were obvious, "if she doesn't lie a lot, why is her nose so long?" That's when I remembered that *Pinocchio* was currently showing at the movie theaters. The kid had looked at my nose and thought of Pinocchio.

But my husband insists that he *likes* my pointed nose. In fact, he insists he likes all the things about my body that I always thought were a problem, as well as the things I always liked about myself (like my hands). He says that the so-called "flaws" are what help make me unique.

His acceptance and appreciation have helped me to accept and appreciate every part of myself. And as I think of him and his appearance, I understand. Because I, too, love everything about him just because it is part of him.

I think that is how God thinks of us. He made us as we are, and he likes us as we are because each of us is unique, and that uniqueness is something he values greatly.

2. *Stop the comparison game.* As Jim Long points out in the following chapter, we are surrounded by images of "beautiful people." Often we dislike our bodies because we compare ourselves with those perfect images.

Who do you use for comparison? Is it the cultural ideal you see in the media everywhere (slim, lithe women with flawless complexions or tall, muscular men with perfect tans and perfect teeth)? Or is it someone specific that you know—the "Jim Patterson" in your life?

3. *Thank God for each item on your list of things you don't like and can't change.* That's right, I said *thank God for it.* Recognize that whatever you're rejecting is a part of the you that God loves. Affirm, out loud, "Thank you, God, for my nose [or whatever you dislike]. I love it because it's part of how you made me, and I'm beautiful to you."

You may gag at this exercise at first, but if you do it with honest appreciation, you'll be surprised at its power.

All the Lovely People

Jim Long

Ever notice how many beautiful people there are? *Most* people are startlingly attractive, ideally proportioned, stunningly outfitted with class and style. Most women exude a luscious sensuality that stirs wild impulses in handsome male hunks (which describes most guys). These perfect people who surround us smile alluringly, revealing straight white teeth and sparkling, fluid eyes. When the guys flex, firm muscles ripple under chic sweaters, impressing perfect females who are round and ample or lean and lithe in all the right places.

Most people are beautiful. I know. I read magazines. Watch television. Catch an occasional movie. Glance at billboards. Obviously, most people are beautiful.

Ever notice how few beautiful people there are? Few are startlingly attractive, ideally proportioned, stunningly outfitted with class and style. Not too many women are round and ample, lean and lithe in all the right places. Few exude a luscious sensuality that stirs wild impulses in firm-muscled male hunks (and there aren't many of those either).

Most people are less than beautiful. I know. I've sat in the school's bleachers, observing the student body filing in for a game. I've sat in bus stations or airline terminals and simply watched people. I have noticed those who stand in line at supermarkets or department stores. I've been to the beach.

How many beautiful people are there? Few. And even most

of the beautiful would point to imperfections, minute or mammoth, that rob them of the security of *feeling* beautiful.

Ever notice what high standards we set for ourselves? We have defined attractiveness so restrictively that we have excluded most people. Ourselves included. Ourselves *excluded*. You must be just the right foot size, nose size, tooth size, lip size, thigh size. We have created a narrow band of beauty, and most of us are outside its limits.

So why do we define beauty with such tight confines? Why can't we observe the wonder of the human body—and the population's diversity!—and call *everyone* beautiful?

To us, gold and jewels are valuable because they are rare. If they were commonplace, we would take them for granted as valueless. Were we dropped into a world of plentiful diamonds, we'd give granite engagement rings. Such an ingrained idea (beauty must be rare) drives us to define beauty so exclusively that most of us are left out.

Ever notice that standards of beauty change from culture to culture, from year to year? One group values an ivory complexion. Another goes for hide tanned under the summer sun (or winter sunlamp). One culture tattoos the face, pierces the nose, or slips discs under the lips to enlarge them. Another paints the face an "embarrassed pink" and pierces the earlobe—once, twice, three times. One group tightly braids the hair, another frees the locks to cascade over the shoulders and down the back. A wet look. A dry look. Heads bushy. Heads shaved. Individually and together we have the ability to choose our definition of beauty. And we *do* choose it. We alter beauty to follow shifting fads (though we keep the limits of attractiveness painfully narrow).

Perhaps it's time to redefine beauty, to give it a broader definition. Maybe physical perfection shouldn't be so restrictive. Maybe we should develop a bit more tolerance for our own appearance and the appearance of others. What would happen if we did? Would we discover physical beauty where we never guessed it existed? And with our preoccupation for physical things diminished, would we suddenly see a beauty that had little to do with things physical?

Ever notice how many beautiful people there are? All of us!

YOUR TURN

Ways I Enjoy Being Physical:

(For instance, using my eyes to bird-watch, using my ears to listen to music, using my legs to hike.)

1. _____
2. _____
3. _____
4. _____
5. _____
6. _____
7. _____
8. _____
9. _____
10. _____

Male and Female: Your Sexuality is Your Own

Tim Stafford

Remember Louie in the first chapter, the tomboy who had trouble liking herself as a girl? Rejecting her feminine identity was one way she rejected herself because she didn't like being who she was. Your sexual identity is probably on your mind when you think of whether or not you like your body. You want to look a certain way in order to appeal to the opposite sex.

A family friend of mine was taking a shower with his tiny daughter one morning when she asked him what the difference was between girls and boys. *I knew we would have this talk sooner or later,* he thought, *but I never thought it would happen so soon.* Embarrassed, he turned the question around.

"What do you think the difference is?" he asked his daughter. Standing stark naked under the running water, he thought the basic differences were obvious. So did his daughter. After a moment's reflection she answered, "The difference is, girls wear shower caps and boys don't." That seemed to be all the discussion she wanted.

At the age of two or three the differences between girls and boys are not terribly problematic. Pure curiosity leads kids to ask, but they don't seem to have a lot of emotion riding on the answer. The parents blush at the subject, but not the kids. A few years later, boys and girls in elementary school don't even act very curious. They define the differences between the sexes so sharply that they hardly want to associate with each other. Most boys think girls are beneath contempt because they cannot throw a ball. Most girls regard boys as savages because they think throwing a ball is so almighty important. Quite voluntarily, the sexes separate.

Then, about the time they enter junior high school, boys and girls experience a radical change, a change they never grow out of. Oddly enough, the differences (physically) become even more obvious. Yet these increasingly different males and females grow increasingly attracted to each other's way of acting. If you don't measure up—if you're not masculine or feminine—you won't end up happily partnered. There are all kinds of unwritten rules. As the sayings go, "Guys don't like girls who are pushy," or, "A guy has to be taller (and older) than the girl he's going with." Girls wait around after school for their guys to get out of basketball practice; a guy who did the same thing for a girl would feel silly. Both guys and girls play their part by the rules, or try to.

Where do these rules come from? They're not written down anywhere. They did not come from heaven like the Ten Commandments. But everybody knows them and, to some extent, believes them. TV embodies them. Burt Reynolds and Dolly Parton caricature them.

Try as you may, you can't entirely escape these stereotypes. Some people say the differences are genetic and some people say they're just cultural. From a practical point of view it doesn't matter too much which group is right. The differences are deeply ingrained into our very sense of life. People have been acting "masculine" and "feminine" for thousands of years, and the very fact that the human race has survived suggests a measure of success for this behavior. Besides, guidelines help us know how to act in emotionally confusing situations.

Still, these masculine and feminine standards inevitably leave us with a lot of anxiety. Nobody really measures up; only one person in one hundred is born with the genetic material to look like "The American Dreamboat"; the rest just try to make up for what God failed to provide. And bear in mind that looks are just the beginning. The differences between males and females are more than physical. Hardly any girl is really soft and submissive right to the very bottom of her heart, and not even Clint Eastwood has absolutely stainless steel skin.

That's why the fashion, cosmetic, and deodorant industries can make so much money out of our worries. Their basic pitch is: "You need all the help you can get to measure up to the ideal. If you buy our clothes (perfume, after-shave, eye shadow, deodorant), at least you won't be messing up in *that* area." Worries of this sort afflict nearly everyone.

STEREOTYPES

I am not exactly knocking the stereotypes. Girls and boys, men and women really are different, and the stereotypes give us some handles on understanding the often incomprehensible differences. The accumulated wisdom of the centuries has something to it. A lot of women *do* respond on a more immediate, emotional level than I do. A lot of women are a great deal better at humanizing a home than I am. A lot of women are gentler than I am. Whether that's so because it is written in our genes, or because they were given dolls to play with while I was given trucks, doesn't matter too much when it comes to getting along together.

Males and females are different, and we want very much to learn to get along together. Any hints we can gather about how to do that are welcome.

What concerns me about the stereotypes is that people sometimes hold them up as a blueprint for a battleship, as though life were made from steel plate. There's no flexibility, no creativity, no individuality. It's as though every man or woman should live by the blueprint, taking the shape that each has been given and bolting one's self into place.

I don't find this a good description of human life. I would rather think of people as living, changeable things—like trees. There are differences between maples and beeches, but each maple and each beech is unique. Each tree changes over the years. Each tree is shaped by the wind and the seasons.

Likewise, each person is unique. Few fit the stereotypes.

FREEDOM IN CHRIST

Our world is a confusing place. Contradictory messages concerning the differences between the sexes get planted in TV and the movies and magazines and everywhere else. They usually are presented not as theories worth consideration, but as well-known facts. Meanwhile, relationships don't last like they once did, and hardly anyone grows up with a secure feeling that someday, somewhere in suburbia he will have a little family of his own, forever. All of this varied bewilderment has a unified effect: It makes people worry about themselves.

Christianity does, I believe, help straighten out this confusion. It offers some fundamental answers—information from the designer himself, information about what human beings really are like. But before that it does something more basic: It sets you free. Christianity does this through three big words of reassurance and challenge: *God made you.* He did not make you in the image of Miss America or Bill Cosby or anybody else. He made you in his own image, and he made you to reflect his character in the unique character you are. You do not, therefore, have to worry that he left out some crucial ingredient. You do not have to feel concern that one of your chromosomes may be missing. The only ideal male or female to measure yourself against is yourself—you as God wants you to be.

A girl who is not by nature pretty and dainty does not have to try to become so. A guy who is not by nature tough does not have to imitate Bruce Springsteen. God's command isn't, "Be a man," or "Be pretty." His command is, "Be thankful," thankful for what he has given you. *God has a wonderful destiny for you.* It isn't as though you are a finished product. God made you what you are, but more important he wants to make you what you need to be. His plan doesn't just include your "spiritual" nature. It includes your physical, emotional, and sexual nature, too.

God can take you where you need to go. If that involves a lifelong marriage, he can suit you to that. If that involves lifelong singleness, he can suit you to that. Your destiny is not written in your genes or in your poor family background. It is written in his Book: Life to any who believe.

To God, the difference between girls and boys is really not that important. "In Christ," Paul wrote, "there is no male or female." He didn't mean that male and female are identical. He meant that in the really important things of life, sexuality isn't even a category. Whether you are a "real man" or a "real woman" doesn't affect your life in Jesus Christ. It may be the thing that gets you branded by society as "good" or "bad," but it will not make much difference in the final analysis. And that's not just "religious" talk; it's talk about reality by someone who knows the meaning of reality because he made it.

In Christ, the question of whether a girl has a mustache or a guy is a jock never comes up. In Christ there is great freedom to know what matters, and to quit worrying about the many things that ultimately don't—including the differences between males and females.

LIVING IN THE GAP

Jesus said again and again: "Don't live for yourself. Die to yourself, and then you can live." To understand this, a person has to start by acknowledging the gap between what he is and what he wants to be—a gap between his ideal of masculinity (or femininity) and what he feels inside himself, a gap between his actual experience of life and the happiness he wishes for himself.

How do you live with this gap? The obvious, most popular answer is to become a pursuer of happiness. You grab as much as you can get of whatever looks good. If it's sex, you're on the make. If it's beauty, you spend your life in a clothing or cosmetic store. If it's an image of masculinity or femininity or androgyny, you fantasize and imitate that image. If it's love, you spend hours dreaming and scheming.

But that is not what it means to follow Christ. He warned us that his followers would have to pick up their crosses each day and follow *him*, not happiness. He warned us that the only way to find life is to give up chasing it and instead, in Jesus' strong words, "die to yourself." What does this say about the difference between girls and guys? Quite simply, that God does not usually dissolve all our problems and anxieties. Our sense of happiness is not a guiding beacon for life; our guiding beacon is Jesus. We want to be faithful to him, and we believe that ultimately he will lead us to true and lasting joy.

A girl who doesn't fit the feminine stereotype may find she is lonely. She wishes to get married but sees no guy on the horizon who appreciates her "unfeminine" traits. She must learn to give her needs and desires to God, trusting that he is at work in her life, even in her loneliness. A guy may feel intense homosexual longings that make him ashamed but won't go away. He must take these longings to God, asking him for the strength to resist them, and allowing the Holy Spirit to work in his life.

Indeed, there will be some pain for every person, and it will be distinctly different for each person. But pain is not a sign that God has abandoned us. Only through that pain can we come to life. Only by living with Christ in our unique and difficult situations will we grow to truly understand ourselves as men and women.

The most valuable insights into how to be a man or a woman—and how to be a human being—come as you live in healthy relationships—first and foremost with God, then with your parents and family, and finally with both male and female friends of your own age. To live well in these relationships you have to stop living for yourself. You have to learn that your own happiness is not the axis on which the earth turns. You have to live with frustration and uncertainty and even with suffering. But if you will turn your attention to others' needs, you will become the man or woman God wants you to be.

YOUR TURN

Finish each sentence, listing the characteristics that come to mind when you think of what being a man or a woman is all about. List both physical and psychological attributes for both sexes.

My idea of a real man . . .

_____

_____

_____

_____

My idea of a real woman . . .

_____

_____

_____

_____

Circle all the words that fit you. Cross out all the words that don't fit you.

Social

*However much we guard our-
selves against it, we tend to shape
ourselves in the image others have
of us. It is not so much the example
of others we imitate, as the
reflection of ourselves in their eyes
and the echo of ourselves in their
words.*

(Eric Hoffer)

Moving Outward: The Social Scene

So far you've been journeying inward, taking a look at who you are and how you feel about yourself. But no one can define himself in a vacuum; other people play a powerful part in how you see yourself.

In this section you will explore several types of people that affect you deeply. You'll recognize them all. First come the labelers, who peg you as a certain type and maybe even reject you for it. Then come the winners, those who seem to have everything; next to them you often feel like a nobody. And what about the opposite sex? How you do or don't succeed with them has a lot to do with your self-image. Finally, your family, especially your parents, has an enormous impact on who you are now and who you will become.

GETTING IN TOUCH WITH YOUR SOCIAL LIFE

This process of being molded by others definitely is *interactive:* You have a lot of control in how you let people affect you. In your journal exercises you'll begin to get a handle on what those other people are doing to you—and how to make your interactions with them a positive part of your personal growth.

How Others See You

Whether you're the biggest jock on campus or the class geek, chances are you have very little idea what you look like to those around you. If only you knew what it was people disliked about you, it would be easier to change, right? Well, here's a quiz that will help you see yourself in a little different light: the way others see you.

After each question is a list of responses. Just circle the letter that would indicate your initial reaction. Don't spend a lot of time thinking about the questions, because there are no right or wrong answers. Be as honest as you can and maybe you'll see a different you.

1. When I get angry I
   a. get nasty and sarcastic but never lose control.
   b. become anxious and upset.
   c. feel frustrated and powerless.
   d. try not to let it show.
   e. scream, rage, and sometimes throw things.
2. I don't understand why
   a. my abilities aren't appreciated more.
   b. everything I do is so complex and difficult.
   c. I never seem to get ahead.
   d. my life is so unexciting.
   e. I can't put my creativity to better use.
3. When others are critical of me I
   a. assure them I have control of the situation.

    b. feel insecure and vulnerable.

    c. always make the situation worse.

    d. try to follow their suggestions.

    e. don't pay any attention.

4. If a very important person came to dinner I'd

    a. try to impress him.

    b. make sure everything was perfect.

    c. end up burning the roast.

    d. plan a formal, appropriate meal.

    e. cook and dress as usual.

5. People say that my best quality is

    a. intelligence.

    b. my eye for details.

    c. my ability to get along with others.

    d. my free spirit.

    e. nothing in particular.

6. The people who attract my attention are always

    a. clever and outspoken.

    b. relaxed in their relationships.

    c. more successful than I am.

    d. people I can use for models.

    e. exciting and far-out.

7. At a party where I don't know anyone I usually

    a. search out an interesting person to talk to.

    b. go home early because I'm so ill at ease.

    c. sit and wait for someone to notice me.

    d. join in any conversation at the first opportunity.

    e. contrive a unique way to attract attention.

8. I am uncomfortable when I

    a. let emotions interfere with reason.

    b. act impulsively.

    c. get involved in a power struggle.

    d. disregard my obligations.

    e. follow in someone else's footsteps.

9. Sometimes people make me feel that I

    a. should keep my ideas to myself.

    b. am preoccupied with trivialities.

    c. cannot live up to their standards.

d. am too good to be real.

e. should be less loud.

10. It upsets me when

a. I am disregarded by others.

b. my problems are scoffed at.

c. people push me around.

d. I don't know what I am supposed to do.

e. I don't have the freedom to express myself.

Your Score: Next to each letter write the number of times you circled that letter. The letter that has the most responses represents an overall characteristic tendency. If you have more than four responses in any one category, that quality probably exists in you. Seven or more in a category means you have strong tendencies in that area.

Letter *a* represents "The Know-it-all"; *b*, "The Worrier"; *c*, "The Loser"; *d*, "The Conformist"; and *e*, "The Rebel."

THE KNOW-IT-ALL

You like to think of yourself as "well-informed," but "big mouth" is the way most people think of you. Thinking you know everything is not the best way to win friends. When you make a mistake it makes people glad you are getting what you deserve.

To stop being a know-it-all, openness is the first point on the agenda. You must try to be more open-minded, realizing that most people can think for themselves. Take other people's ideas just as seriously as you do your own. Work *with* others, not against them.

THE WORRIER

You can tell yourself that you "care more about the little things" than others do, but to your friends you are a worrywart, someone who constantly wrings your hands over something.

To change, you must realize that most things are not worth the energy worrying expends. You've got to learn to make the best of your mistakes and not be afraid to fail now and then. Usually, that is what is really causing you to worry: your fear of failure.

THE LOSER

You've somehow gotten it into your mind that winning is wrong. You are programmed to lose. You might blame it on bad luck, but your friends see it as a self-destruct mechanism. You've learned to live with failure because there is something you fear much more than failing. Find out what you fear and you'll be on the way to becoming a new person.

THE CONFORMIST

You see yourself as "one of the gang"; your friends see you as dull. You try to remain safe in every area of your life, taking no risks, but it is stifling you. Try something new, check out your fear of the unknown. Deliberately break with your old way of doing things. Your friends will notice the change and you will become a much more interesting person.

THE REBEL

You may consider yourself outspoken, but to those around you, you're a troublemaker. Everybody seems to know what you're against, but nobody knows what you are for. You probably don't know yourself.

Instead of always tearing things down, try some building up. You can express yourself in positive ways if you work at it. Learning to compromise would be a start. You won't lose respect if you do.

YOUR TURN

What's your label? In a sense, the quiz you just took isn't fair. It stuck a label on you. You have many more dimensions than the quiz could acknowledge.

Unfortunately, other people do tend to slap labels on us. In that sense, the quiz was accurate. We have to deal with labels in our social relations.

LABELS OTHERS HAVE PINNED ON ME:

_____

_____

_____

_____

_____

_____

_____

_____

_____

Which of these labels still hurt? Put a check by them. Which of these labels have lost their sting? Put a smiling face by them.

Feeling Rejected

Jim Long

What happens when others label you and then reject you? Maybe you wear your hair in a particular style and someone labeled you a punker because of it. Then you discovered there are a lot of people in the world for whom "punker" is a dirty word. Or maybe a certain group of kids who witnessed a particular experience of yours never let you live it down; you are forever branded a "wimp" because you refused to get involved in a fight, or whatever. No matter where it comes from, rejection is painful. In the following article Jim Long helps us understand and cope with rejection.

The sun did not merely shine, it spread its rays like fingers and covered the sky with its palm. And there, sweltering under the onslaught of early summer, we gathered for P.E. I hated it. I knew it was Monday afternoon, and that was when we would choose teams. I had considered staying home sick or cutting class. Instead, I was there, standing at the edge of the group, watching it shrink as the valuable guys lined up in the order of their importance behind two captains making important decisions.

"I'll take McKenzie."

"I want Jeff."

"Reggie."

Pause. "Uh . . . , Hamilton, I guess."

Longer pause.

I couldn't look up. If you look your friend in the eye and he sees you and still passes you up, the rejection hurts more. Instead, look down. Stare at the heels of Larry's Nikes. Look down and be thankful that, for now, there is something standing in front of you. A shield. Because in a few moments there won't be. Twenty-three of the twenty-seven guys who were standing on this side of the field will be standing on that side, looking on, advising the captains of the liabilities of the remaining four. And then there will be three, then two, and then one. Countdown.

REJECTION

So you're the last one picked for gym class. Or you're cut from the team. You run for student government and lose, or try out for cheerleader and don't make it. You ask someone out and she turns you down. That person who seems so neat never even notices you. Your parents fight and you figure in some odd way it must be your fault. They divorce and you're not sure which one you belong to or if anyone even cares.

How do you handle feelings of rejection? How do you even understand those feelings?

I recall the questions that came to mind when my brother and I couldn't get along, or when my father was impatient with me. There might have been dozens of expressions of their care and love, but at the moment of anger or impatience all I could see was rejection.

I once stood in the rain with a girl I cared for as she struggled to say tactfully, "I want to break off our relationship but still be friends." In retrospect, I see what a good friendship it might have been. At the time, I saw only rejection.

And now, as I think of rejection—my gym class fiasco, my father's anger or discipline, my brother's disagreement, my girlfriend's declaration of independence—I realize that rejection comes in different styles. Though the hurt feelings are similar, the rejection experiences are varied.

Sometimes I *feel* rejected when I have not been rejected at all. I feel rejected because I am insecure and things didn't quite drift in my direction. I feel snubbed but I wasn't really put off—I just wasn't pampered. My script for life called for me to be center stage throughout the production, but the director sent me out to sell popcorn.

Sometimes I feel rejected because I am pitched into a game where the options are severely limited from the outset. There'll be only one student-body president. But a vote *for* the other candidate is not necessarily a vote *against* me. It may merely be a vote for the other person. The ballots are cast and counted, and I come up short. If only one person can win and I lose, perhaps feeling rejected is not quite the proper response. It's not that I am rejected, it's that the other person is selected. There is a difference. The same may be true of being cut from the team, not making cheerleader, not making first chair in the band, or being someone's friend but not their *best* friend.

Even so, it feels like rejection.

And sometimes it is.

Jerry was one of my closest friends in high school, but Jerry had a violent temper. And when he was ticked, he was irrational. I remember the evening he lost his temper with Sherri, his girlfriend. It was a stupid, inconsequential disagreement, but Jerry's face flushed in anger. He breathed like a snorting bull; he yelled and cussed. But he was wrong.

I had overheard it all and as he stomped off toward the car I tried to reason with him. *I'll be the peacemaker,* I thought. But Jerry wouldn't listen to a word of reason. He leaped in the car, squealed away from the curb, and tore off down the highway. Sherri and I looked at each other, both flabbergasted. Then we watched as Jerry made a U-turn and roared back down the highway toward us. His Ford thundered past. Then he turned around again and flashed past us, down the block. Another U-turn. Again. And again. With each pass, his speed increased and his control of the car decreased.

It was monumentally irrational, but being concerned about Jerry's safety (and not concerned enough about my own), and wanting to be the hero that would bring reconciliation to such a silly dispute, I shrugged off my earlier rejection, stepped into the street, walked into Jerry's lane, and tried to flag him down. *Naturally,* I told myself, *Jerry will stop and I can cool him down.* But Jerry didn't stop, and I almost danced with his radiator.

I went home that night angry, but baffled, too, by the intensity of Jerry's rage. Then even stronger feelings settled in the pit of my stomach: feelings of rejection. I had gone out of my way to be a friend to Jerry, to help him save face with Sherri, and he had treated me like trash. I felt rejected even though Jerry was obviously at fault.

And I observe: Feeling rejected, or being rejected, does not necessarily mean that you are wrong. Sometimes it simply illustrates how inappropriate, or even wrong, someone else is. Maybe they feel uneasy, even guilty, for their wrongness. They're frustrated and, wrong as it is, blowing steam at you is their way of depressurizing their temper.

I watched as one high-school group ridiculed a spastic classmate. The girl walked funny and couldn't quite coordinate her hands. But she had the same delicate feelings as anyone, and those feelings were violated. Simply put, an entire group's values can stink. They may accept one person and reject another for the wrong reasons—because they figure the person looks a bit odd, or thinks a bit too differently, or wears J.C. Penneys instead of Calvins.

In rejecting someone based on their appearance, we are making a stronger statement about ourselves than we are about the one we reject. Acceptance and rejection are windows of our values.

Still, even if the other person is the guilty party, rejection hurts. How do you handle it? I wish I could write as long a list on how to cope with rejection as I could of instances of feeling rejected, but I can't. I *can* however, share a few thoughts that have helped me put rejection in perspective.

Separate feelings of rejection from the reality of rejection. Is someone really trying to put you down, or are the circumstances just taking a different turn than you would have chosen? Or have you merely dreamed up the rejection idea in your own paranoid head? Ask yourself what really is happening. Self-centeredness can so easily creep into your life. Almost without knowing it, you can become the self-appointed traffic cop of your relationships. It's as if you brandish a badge and dominate the friendship. Then, when people tire of being dominated and don't yield the right of way, you feel rejected. If you cultivate the ability to see yourself and your relationships through other people's eyes you can avoid these kinds of problems.

If you really are being rejected, face the obvious question: Why? Your mind plays funny tricks on you. If pressed to choose, you almost invariably assume the rest of the world is rotten, not you. Sometimes, however, people look at you and see snobbishness, pride, or cantankerousness. Maybe you are boisterous or gross, or have bad breath. Rejection can sometimes send you a valuable signal: You need to change.

Remember the idea of limited options. Don't take it personally when you don't make the team, or win the election, or get picked first. Rather, cultivate a spirit of congratulating others in their success. That will be much better received than sulking because of your shortcomings.

Consider the possibility that the other person or group is expecting the wrong things. Are you the victim of someone's wrong values? People may be expecting you to party, but it doesn't square with your values. They figure you're funny if you don't wear brand names, but it just isn't that crucial to you. Or you're short on money, and they value people with endless resources. Just because people are looking for "beautiful" friends, and in their eyes you're middle-of-the-road average, it doesn't mean they're right and you're wrong. Often, it's the other way around.

Realize that certain circumstances are both wrong and unchangeable. I'm sure you'll agree that people place too much importance on beauty, strength, athletic inclinations, or innate brilliance. It is unfair to the majority of us average people. But the likelihood of single-handedly changing society's values is slim— even skinny. Learning to cope with feelings of rejection often starts with the hard realization that there are certain things you will never be able to change. Then you must begin the lifelong struggle to learn contentment.

The answer to rejection is not always to pursue acceptance; sometimes that would be wrong—other times, impossible.

Remember how rejection feels and determine that you will not inflict those feelings on others. When you feel the pain of rejection, it is very easy to walk away and then, in your frustration, pass the pain on to others.

Jesus told a story once about a man who had a huge debt. Had he worked his life away, he would have been unable to pay it off. And so, facing imprisonment, he begged for mercy and the debt was canceled. So this man, free of his indebtedness, walked off scot-free. But as he walked down the street, he met an old friend who owed him some pocket change. Forgetting his own feelings—and the forgiveness of his own indebtedness—only minutes before, he decided to put the screws to his penny-ante debtor. He would not even consider his friend's plea for mercy.

The difficult circumstances you endure often are prime opportunities to learn the good lesson of how to treat others. If you are sensitive to what God can teach you through hard times, you can reach out to others when they face similar circumstances and help them, rather than compound the problem.

Dealing with Winners

LaVonne Thompson
(as told to Ruth Senter)

Is isn't just the rejecters who make us feel small. Just think about what happens to our self-image when other people seem better than we are. How can we deal with the "winners"? They themselves may never reject us—but they can make us reject ourselves. The following story is by someone who experienced, firsthand, the conflicts of trying to deal with a winner.

The minute I saw her I knew there'd be trouble between us. Wendi. Beautiful. Blue-eyed. Perfect complexion. I first saw her by my locker outside homeroom 3-A. She wore yellow clothes that looked like they'd come right out of *Seventeen*—yellow was my favorite color.

Her fingers were long and thin. A piano player, no doubt. I pounded out Rachmaninoff with thick stubs, and strained to reach an octave.

Advanced calculus. Did it have to be on top of her book pile? Everyone knew advanced calculus was not for high school juniors. I'd barely survived algebra. Around school, brains and beauty didn't usually mix. Except for Wendi.

My world was eroding. Wendi had invaded my territory. She was standing in front of *my* locker, talking and laughing with *my* friends, about to enter *my* homeroom. It was as though she had walked right past some invisible No Trespassing sign I had posted to protect my domain. I'd invested time and energy in those friendships. Who wouldn't be protective?

Suddenly I felt I had to try harder, and for the next nine months I did. Whenever Wendi was around I talked louder, laughed more, told more jokes, counted friends, calculated every move.

Everywhere I went, she haunted me like a phantom. When she turned up at Jake's Pizza one Friday night after a football game with a guy I had dated, I immediately tallied up our scores. Who was friendlier, better-dressed, a better conversationalist, most fun—the all-around best? Wendi *always* came out the winner.

The hardest contest of all was the senior-class election. Steve and I had been a president/vice president team all through high school. I thought things would stay the same. But that was before Wendi. The final countdown was on. Posters. Promises. Election speeches. Platform politics. I rolled the pages of my speech into a two-inch cylinder and stared into the audience of next year's seniors. They were my friends. So why did I feel I had to prove myself? Where was my confidence? Wendi, sitting next to me, was to speak next. Why was that such a threat?

"I'm scared," she whispered to me before she rose. Wendi scared? Poised, confident, in-control Wendi? But she really was— the typed pages in her hand were shaking. She squeezed my arm as though for support, then stepped to the microphone. Suddenly I saw a side of Wendi I'd never even thought about. It had never occurred to me to think about her feelings.

It wasn't easy to lose the election to Wendi. Now she had the seniors' official stamp of approval. No one knew she was scared; no one except me. I knew what it felt like to be scared. I had been scared ever since that first day when I saw her by my locker. Suddenly it was our similarities that mattered, not our differences.

Wendi didn't become opponent-turned-friend overnight. It took a long time before I could relax and stop performing when I was around her. For months, the scoreboard kept blinking in my mind whenever we were together. I kept trying to outdo her. But the more I learned about Wendi the more I liked her, and the less threatened I felt. Gradually I forgot about where I stood in comparison. I began to feel we were standing together—laughing, studying, cheering, talking, even crying together. There was no reason why we couldn't each be strong personalities. Both of us could be good at what we did; we could date the same guys sometimes, have the same friends, and go to the same places without one of us coming up the loser. There was no reason why we had to compete at all. There was room for us both.

Watching a winner is sometimes hard to take. It probably always will be for me. Wendi is definitely a winner. She won a political science award at the end of our junior year, and now dreams about being a U.S. senator. I know, because in one of her braver moments she told me about it. Wendi could win a Senate seat, I'm sure. And I suppose if she should ever run, I would ask to manage her campaign.

YOUR TURN

Competitors?

The person who threatens my sense of being an okay person the

most is _____

_____

Have you ever seen a human, vulnerable side to that person?

When? _____

_____

The situations I feel competitive in are _____

_____

_____

_____

_____

The reason competition affects me so much is (I'm afraid of
losing, I long for glory, etc.)_____

_____

Finding Yourself— Regardless of What People Think

Because rejection is so painful and competition so difficult, we often do everything we can to fit in. Somehow a group helps us cement our identity. There's nothing wrong with the desire to belong—unless it gets out of hand. Sometimes we end up compromising our own individuality. The balance between belonging and losing yourself is not easy to strike, as Stacey, the girl in the next article, discovered.

THAT'S STACEY!

Whenever I walk into the Picadilly Cafeteria, where I work part-time, I'm reminded of another cafeteria—the one at my school, where so many of my identity struggles found their expression. I can still picture the black crowd seated in the far right corner of the room, and me carrying my tray, wondering whether I should sit with them or with the white students.

Over the past few years I've had to figure out not only who I am as a black person, but also how I should fit in with different groups of people.

I attended a private elementary school that was all black with only three white kids. I never treated them any differently from the black kids; it never occurred to me to do so. My parents brought me up to believe that all people are equal but just different, that nobody is less or more of a person than I am. Then, in seventh grade, I went to a public junior high school. I automatically assumed that I'd be able to have both black and white friends, but I soon discovered that no one else agreed with me. Everyone belonged to a clique or in-group that was either all white or all black.

Though I wanted badly to fit in somewhere, I didn't want to be exclusive. I tried to be friends with both groups. When I hung around with the white kids, I acted as "white" as possible—articulating my words carefully, wearing their kind of clothes, listening to their music. And when I hung around with the black crowd, I acted "black."

To my sad surprise, neither group accepted me. Instead, each snubbed me for hanging around with the other group. I'm sure they must have sensed that I was simply trying to impress them and gain their approval. I felt hurt and frustrated, but I didn't know what to do about it. I began to think that it wasn't possible to have both black and white friends. Yet I still wanted to fit in somewhere.

In the eighth grade, I decided to devote all my energies to making it in the black crowd. I did everything I could to conform. Yet there were so many unwritten expectations that anyone who was black had to fill. For one thing, a black person had to dress very sharp and wear designer clothes at all times. Guys, for example, might have been expected to wear immaculate, unfaded Sergio Valente jeans (dry-cleaned and pressed with a seam), a dress shirt, and a thin knit or leather tie. Girls wore bright-colored miniskirts with matching stockings, even in winter.

Like the others, I fixed my radio dial to the soul stations and got into the Commodores, Marvin Gaye, Rick James, Prince, and Rose Royce. When I went on dates, I'd stay out real late and go to the dance at the village hall. There a DJ would play great dance music, and about 100 to 150 people—all black—would show up. I still enjoy those dances, but back then I went only because it was the cool thing to do.

I was even expected to talk a certain way, using incomplete sentences and lots of black phrases. For instance, virtually everyone in the black crowd had a nickname, usually a shortened form of their middle name. Some people went by names such as Pee Wee, Sweet Leo (or whatever your zodiac sign might be), Smurf or Smurfette. All of this was difficult for me, because both my parents were college professors and had brought me up to speak standard English. But I tried to blend in any way I could.

I suppose I knew that I was compromising myself a little, but I figured it was worth it if I could gain some acceptance. Well, I soon discovered it wasn't worth it. Even when I cast all my votes with the blacks, they refused to accept me. One day during lunch period I strolled into the cafeteria and over to the "black tables." The understood rule was that people sitting at black tables were not to socialize with those at white tables, and vice versa. As I approached the black table, I overheard several people talking about me, saying I was a two-faced snob and, worst of all, calling me an Oreo—black on the outside but white on the inside.

To be called an Oreo by fellow blacks is on a par with being called "nigger" by whites. When someone calls me a nigger, I can't explain how terrible it feels. It just cuts to the bone. I can hardly think of a worse thing to call someone—except perhaps an Oreo. No one knew how deeply it hurt me to be called that.

Since I had failed to make it with the black crowd, I felt miserable and soon looked for another group to hang around with. I found a group made up of both blacks and whites who all had one thing in common: drugs. I knew these people didn't have the morals my parents taught me to have, but I hung around with them anyway. Though I avoided the drugs, I kept up the appearances. My view of the drug crowd changed, however, after I went to one of their Halloween parties. The mother of one of the girls let us have the party at her house and even agreed to buy liquor for the occasion. I could hardly believe it; the other kids just said she was cool. So everyone was drinking themselves silly, and I just watched and talked with one of the girls I had befriended.

When the mother left a while later, almost everyone dashed up the stairs to the bedroom. Even in ninth grade, I was pretty naïve, so I went upstairs to see for myself what was going on. The bedroom door was closed, so I knocked. No answer. I opened it and looked into the semidarkness. I couldn't believe what I saw. There must have been nineteen people sprawled out on a king-sized waterbed, all in various states of undress, climbing all over each other. I stood there for a moment, dumbfounded. Then I quickly shut the door, went downstairs, and cried. The whole scene made me sick. As I sat on the living-room sofa, I felt terribly out of place. I didn't belong at this party. And I didn't belong in this group.

Yet I hadn't found *any* group in which I felt comfortable. It seemed that anyone I hung around with expected me to conform. I could never just be myself—whoever that was. After that party I made a decision: I was going to be the person *I* wanted to be. I would dress however I liked and talk to whomever I wanted—whether they were black or white. I would listen to the music I liked and go to places I wanted to go. Selling out to the crowd just wasn't worth it. I knew I'd rather be a loner for the rest of my life; at least I would be a happy loner.

I wasn't prepared for what happened to me during the months that followed my decision. I made a real attempt to be an individual. I talked with both black and white people, and listened to all different kinds of music—just because I wanted to. Gradually, I felt more and more content with myself. To my surprise, I even began to make a few friends . . . then a few more, and then a few more. Before long I realized that I had more friends than I'd had when I was trying so hard to be like everyone else. The only problem, however, was that all my new friends were white. I hadn't tried to work it that way; it just happened. I had a few black acquaintances, but no real black friends who came over to my house or spent time with me.

One evening during my sophomore year, some black friends of my parents' came over and brought with them two of their daughters. The girls had graduated from my high school a few years earlier, and though I didn't see them very often, we were good friends. I told them a little about my frustration with the black and white crowds at high school. They knew exactly what I was talking about. Soon one of the girls asked me, "Have you ever gone to Campus Life?"

"No," I said. "What's that?"

"Oh, Stacey," they both said together, "you've gotta get into Campus Life. That's where you meet nice people—the kind of people you should hang around with."

Sure, why not? I thought. *I certainly don't have anything to lose.* "OK, maybe I'll give it a try," I told them. So I asked around until I found out when the next Campus Life event would take place. When I learned that a roller-skating party was scheduled, I decided to go since I'm a pretty good skater. Though I was tempted to call a friend to go with me, I ended up taking a bus to the skating rink by myself. I walked in and paid for my skates, and then looked around.

I had never seen anything like it. There were white people and black people and Hispanics and other races all mixed together, having a good time. During that evening I found I could walk up to most anyone, say hi and start a conversation, and not worry that they would ignore me, call me a dirty name, or offer me drugs. I had such a different feeling about these people, a feeling I had never experienced before. When I got home that night, I ran to my parents and told them about the fun I'd had. They were just as excited as I was, so I continued attending Campus Life meetings and events. They just got better and better.

Though no one had told me ahead of time that the organization had religious ties, I found myself eagerly listening to the talks that Jeff, one of the staff people, offered at each meeting. He said that God cares about each of us individually, and that God accepts us as we are. I had always been a moral person and a believer of sorts—I went to church if I could get myself up on Sunday morning—but this stuff about individuality and acceptance struck a chord in me.

Later I attended a Bible study with some other kids. The leader read a passage, and then asked us to go around and say what it meant to us. The comments everyone made surprised me. Each person applied the Bible to his or her own life in a unique way. I half expected everyone to give the same answer or interpretation. I was still suspicious that I would be required to fit into a Christian mold just as I had been expected to conform to all of the other groups. I left that meeting with a sense of relief, and a feeling of confidence in Campus Life—and ultimately in Christianity. I had finally found a close-knit group to belong to, yet I could be an individual at the same time. I could still be myself.

Now, as a senior in high school, I've made many good friends. I'm happy because I genuinely like these people; I'm no longer trying to impress them or gain their approval like I did back in eighth grade. I like myself now, and because I like myself I find that

I like other people more. I still have many more white friends than black. What's funny, though, is that my two very best friends are neither white nor black—one is East Indian (from Pakistan) and the other is Puerto Rican. My parents tease me about it, but they think it's great and so do I.

Around school I've gained sort of a reputation for being different, but people don't see it as a negative thing. (For example, I like to wear unusual clothes. Yesterday I wore a bright red corduroy miniskirt, a large black and white checkered T-shirt, and a pair of plain white Keds that I had painted with different colored checks in acrylic paints.) People stop me in the hall and say, "What is that you're wearing?" Yet they don't mean it as a put-down. They see it as my own way of expressing my individuality.

Instead of sneering at how strange and different I am, they just chuckle and say, "Yup—that's Stacey."

YOUR TURN

How Different Are You?

List all the ways you are different from other people your age:

_____

_____

_____

_____

_____

_____

_____

_____

Put a plus sign (+) by the differences you think are positive.

Put a minus sign (−) by the differences you think are negative.

Put a check by the differences you think are related to your personal or Christian values.

It's easy to *say* we should feel OK about all the ways we're different. But sometimes it still hurts not to belong, regardless of the fact that we know we're right for holding on to our standards. That's when it helps tremendously to find a group of friends who share the same basic values you do, friends who will let you be free to be you. Stacey found such a group in Campus Life.

The need to belong is a legitimate need; God created us to need other people and we don't really find ourselves except in relationship to others. So if you don't have a group that gives you a sense of belonging without compromising your beliefs, find one. Campus Life, Student Venture, Young Life, a church group—all can help you get involved with other young people who share your basic values and will help you become the person God wants you to be.

It also helps to have a few close friends, people with whom you can share some of your more personal thoughts and feelings. In the next chapter, we'll take a look at your friend life, how it's helping (or not helping) you to become the kind of person you want to be.

Friends:
We Need Them

Jim Long

Loneliness is one of the most painful emotions we can feel. We go to great lengths to avoid it. Why do we seem to need friends so much? We all have a need to be understood, to be accepted for who we are. We look to our friends for that, in large measure. (Family members are *supposed* to love us for who we are, so sometimes we discount their acceptance as obligation. Or some of us never have that kind of acceptance from our family.)

Good friends, those who accept you and allow you to be open with your true thoughts and feelings, help you know who you are. Sometimes the only way to figure out what you're really thinking or feeling, or to work through a problem or a decision, is to talk things out with a friend. Keeping a journal is good, but talking things over with a good friend is ten times better!

A good friend can help you see your faults. He or she can tell you when you're being obnoxious, and you can accept the criticism because you believe the person really is telling you for your own good. Also, because your friend accepts you, warts and all, you are better able to accept yourself. Your friends help you realize your values, and sometimes they reshape them. If you hang around people who share your basic values in a positive way, you'll face fewer situations in which you'll feel pressured to go against what you think is right.

If, on the other hand, you hang around with people who don't really accept you as you are, you'll experience inner turmoil. Often you will feel conflict between doing what your friends want to do and doing what you really want to do. You can end up compromising yourself, and eventually reach the point of wondering who you *really* are. ("If I really don't believe in getting drunk, why do I keep drinking at parties?")

Friendship levels. Not all friendships are what you might call "deep." There are different levels of friendship, and each level gives us something. Some friendships share only silly little facts:

"How was the concert?"

"Fine, thanks."

"How was the weather?"

"Fine, thanks."

"Get over your cold?"

"Cold? You must be thinking of Julie."

SLF (Silly Little Fact) friendships are OK—they beat people wishing you a rotten day—but they don't affect our identity much; we have very little invested in them.

Some friendships share profound ideas. It's great to stay up late and solve the problems of the world with a wise friend or two. And sometimes your own junior varsity problem-solving sessions can be as productive as the big-league summit meetings. There's a place for PI (Profound Ideas) friendships. Even if your ideas aren't exactly profound, it's good to have people with whom you can talk about things that interest you. Such friends can help you know what you really think and believe.

But you also need a few friendships that go beyond the swapping of profound ideas. These are friendships that share deep secret feelings. OK, maybe it sounds corny. But when you are uptight, you need someone who understands—someone who can help you unravel your twisted feelings. Someone who listens and cares. When your emotions are so volatile you're sure you cannot hold together, you need someone who will not blush if you unexpectedly find yourself in tears, or run if you start yelling. You don't need many SF (Secret Feelings) friendships, but life is smoother with at least one.

YOUR TURN

List Them:

Silly Little Facts Friends

_____

_____

_____

Profound Ideas Friends

_____

_____

_____

Secret Feelings Friends

_____

_____

_____

On a scale of 1 to 10, how satisfied are you with your friend life?

The Trouble With Guys

Lynn Powulski

Beyond friendship, there's the dating game. How we do—
or don't—succeed with the opposite sex has a lot to do with
our sexual self-image.

There's a problem, though: according to some girls, the
dating game is more like a hunting game, and the guys have
all the weapons; the guys, on the other hand, look mystified and
say it can't be all their fault. So who's right? Sample the strong
opinions in the following article and then you'll have a chance
to respond yourself.

Girls are hunted. If you don't believe me, just watch the guys
when a girl walks into a room. Watch them check out the human
equivalent of an antler spread and assign her a ranking. Watch
them ogle the girl they think is the best trophy, calculating their
odds at bringing her down. Watch the girls huddle together,
waiting for the hunters to single them out. Cavemen clubbed and
carried off their women. Has anything changed?

Of course, I'm exaggerating. But I resent being ogled by a guy
just because I have long hair and a female shape. If a guy really
were looking at *me*, seeing me as a unique person, that might be
different. Then I might feel complimented. But the fact is, I'm
being judged by the *shell* I carry around, doused with lemon rinse,
cheek blusher, and eye shadow. I could be a mannequin for all guys
care!

I don't want to make a big deal out of nothing. But every few years we hear a new cycle of speeches about how *today's* modern youth accept each other as persons, not as objects. Hogwash! Flip through any recent copy of *Seventeen* or *Glamour* and tell me what's changed. Girls are still at the wrong end of the gun barrel. I can't speak for every high school, but I know it's still that way in mine.

Not that girls aren't important. Every guy wants to have one to keep—like a pet. Guys want a girl to tell their problems to, to cuddle up with, to show off to their friends. But we don't quite make it into the human realm. This is made clear when, after taking their dates home, the guys get together again by them-selves. Girls are good for some things, but when it comes to normal, earthy conversation, they're better left at home.

As long as I'm spreading blame around, I'll take some too. We girls constantly fear not having a date, as if the whole world revolved around guys. If you do land a date (thrill!), it doesn't prove you're a fascinating person. Girls trying to attract a guy don't do a lot of extra reading so they'll be interesting to talk to. They don't worry that he knows they're good at writing, or art, or a sport. They worry about how they look. What else counts in attracting a guy? Your self-worth revolves around your looks.

Guys don't seem to have this problem. They can be jocks, they can be smart, they can be into music or art, they can be interested in school politics. If they don't comb their hair in a week, it's more likely considered "cute" than anything else. They have the freedom to express themselves in a great number of ways. A girl has to be a double winner. It isn't enough to be yearbook editor or a school officer or play a great jazz clarinet. If she isn't good-looking she's nothing.

Girls need places where they can be admired, where they can achieve something, where they can talk to other kids on a personal basis. They need chances to be more than bodies.

We girls need to stop believing the lie that we're nothing without a guy. As long as we treat guys as though they are as necessary as oxygen, guys will continue to act like "God's gift." But if we stop acting like Bambi, maybe they'll stop acting like hunters.

YOUR TURN

A Game? Or a Relationship?

My biggest frustration in relating to the opposite sex is

_____

When it comes to women taking the initiative, I think

_____

I think guys should

_____

I think girls should

_____

My worst experience with the opposite sex was

_____

My best experience with the opposite sex was

_____

When Sex Takes Control

If you already have a boyfriend or girlfriend, other issues arise. Sometimes it's wonderful; that person somehow makes you feel more secure than you've ever felt before. But often a wonderful relationship goes sour. Sometimes, as you'll see in the following story, things get "out of control."

It didn't start out to be a serious relationship, but then I guess relationships seldom do.

We met through some friends at school, right at the end of my freshman year. I thought Flint was cute. His name reminded me of a hero in one of those gothic romances, but I liked it.

I was a little surprised when he called one day in the middle of June and asked me out for a pizza. I had a good time, and a few days later he called again.

We ate a lot of pizzas that summer. We saw a few movies together, and we took long walks in the park, where we fed the ducks and sat on a bench and kissed a little. As the weeks went by, I decided I was falling in love.

When school started again, I saw Flint every day. He met me between classes, and we ate lunch together. He even walked me home from school.

I began to notice that I didn't have as much time for the things that had always been so important to me, such as my studies and my tennis practice. My old friends started to dwindle away; I just couldn't find the time to keep up the contact. Flint and I were always together.

I didn't mind the changes enough to do anything about them. I liked Flint. There was something comfortable and nice about having a guy who thought I was so special.

The weather began to get too cold for walks in the park, so we went to his house after school. Since his parents were at work, we were alone to sit on the couch and make out. To begin with, we just kissed and hugged. Then we started petting. Before too many weeks passed, our afternoon sessions got pretty heavy.

Winter came. And one day—January 19th, to be exact—we stopped at Flint's house after a cold, snowy trek home from school. I took off my coat and was heading for the family room when he took my hand and said, "I think we could get warmer if we went upstairs to my room."

I knew what he meant.

"I don't think we should," I said, starting for the family room again.

He followed and stopped me. He said it would improve our relationship, that it would give us a chance to show how much we really loved each other.

I wasn't convinced.

When I still hesitated, Flint asked, "Why shouldn't we?"

I couldn't think of a good reason. After all the heavy petting we'd done, it did seem like the next step.

We stood there for what seemed like an hour. I never actually said yes, but when Flint took my hand again I followed him upstairs. I went home that day feeling both guilty and disappointed. I figured that was because it was my first time.

A few days later we had sex again. Soon it was a regular part of our routine—but I felt it was wrong and the guilt began building inside me.

I'd been lying a lot to my parents since I had begun stopping at Flint's after school. Those lies didn't bother me much at first, but once we started having sex the lies weighed heavier and heavier on my conscience.

Other things bothered me, too.

The more sex we had, the more that seemed to be all we did.

Oh, we still went out. We still did a lot of the same things together. But somehow everything was different. Everything seemed to revolve around the sex. It was like sex *was* the relationship.

We still talked. We just never really said anything. Sex became our communication, but I didn't want it to be that way.

Something else began to bother me. Flint very quickly became more and more possessive of my time. When I planned to go to a mall or out to McDonald's with friends, he accused me of not wanting to spend the time with him. We had big arguments about that, but I almost always gave in and dropped my other plans.

Sometimes I really enjoyed Flint's possessive streak. He had a way of acting proud of me when we were in public. I remember when spring came and I went to his first baseball game. He called me over to the fence before the game to give me a big kiss and promise to hit a home run just for me. It was such a corny scene that I had to laugh. Yet I felt good that Flint wanted to show everybody in the stands how crazy he was about me.

Unfortunately, the good times didn't erase the guilt and unhappiness I felt about our physical relationship. I vowed to myself a couple times that I was going to draw some new lines, but I discovered it was impossible to shift our relationship into reverse. The times I tried to call a halt to the sex, Flint would demand to know why I was saying no when I'd said yes the time before. He acted so hurt and confused, my resolve quickly faded—but my guilt and unhappiness didn't.

When I started my junior year, one of my friends invited me to a Campus Life club meeting. I enjoyed it so much that I went back the next week, despite Flint's objections. I remember thinking, *Maybe this Christianity stuff is a solution to my problems.* Yet going to those meetings, being with the people there and hearing the discussions about God, made me feel even more guilty and unhappy with the way my life was going.

At the close of one meeting the leader talked about how a person who turns his or her life over to God can feel a real sense of inner peace. I thought, *That's what I need, peace. I'm so torn up, so unhappy with myself. I want that peace.* Then the guy closed the meeting with prayer and asked anyone who wanted to get to know God and God's peace to raise a hand. I did, but I pulled it back down quickly, hoping no one saw it.

He asked those who had raised a hand to talk to one of the staff people after the meeting. I didn't stay. Yet, for the first time I seriously considered breaking up with Flint. Once I even hinted to him that I didn't think our relationship was going very well.

He launched into a mushy speech about how much he loved and needed me and how we just needed to keep working at our love. For the entire week after that he was so loving, sweet, and unpossessive that I began to think things were starting to change.

Two incidents showed me that wasn't true.

One night we started talking about the future. I said I was beginning to think I'd like to go to college out West if I could find a school that offered a strong journalism program and that could give me a shot at winning at least a partial tennis scholarship. Flint got a terribly stricken look on his face and told me if I really loved him I wouldn't consider anything other than going to the local community college so I could be near him.

I dropped the subject at that point, but his response ate at me for days. It didn't seem to matter to him that I'd planned on a journalism career since I was twelve, or that intercollegiate tennis had been one of my goals for longer than that.

Crisis point number two came a few weeks later. Flint called just as I was heading out the door to pick up a couple of girlfriends for roller-skating.

"Who are you going with?" he wanted to know.

"Just Phyllis and Karen."

I couldn't believe his next words or the sudden anger I could read between them.

"You can't go!" he snapped.

"Why not?" I snapped back.

"Because I don't want you skating in front of all the guys at the rink if I'm not with you."

I still couldn't believe what I was hearing. "I'm going, like it or not!" I shouted, and slammed the receiver into the cradle.

But Flint lives just a block from Phyllis, and when I pulled into her driveway, he was there. As Phyllis slid in on the passenger side, Flint and I continued a humiliating and heated discussion.

After I steadfastly refused to give up my plans, he suddenly switched demands.

"Then I want you to call me as soon as you get home!"

"That's stupid," I argued. "It'll be after midnight."

"I'll be up waiting for your call."

"Then you'll still be up for breakfast. I'm not calling."

At that he walked behind the car, folded his arms, and declared he wasn't moving until I promised to call.

Phyllis was trying to pretend she wasn't hearing any of this, and I felt like crawling under the seat. "OK, I'll call," I conceded. He moved, I backed out of the driveway, and took off.

Late that night, after I'd gotten home and dutifully reported in to Flint, I lay in bed and tried to forget the entire embarrassing evening. It was then that the thought struck me: My life wasn't my own anymore. Somewhere, somehow, I'd lost control.

I'd given Flint my body, my emotions, and most of my time—and he still wanted more. He even wanted to possess my future.

That night was the final turning point. I knew I had to get out.

I couldn't have been more determined. Yet I couldn't break things off on my own. More than ever before I sensed my own hopelessness and limitations, and I sensed a need for God's help in running my life. At the next Campus Life meeting I decided to become a Christian.

Even then I struggled. Every day for a month I prayed for the strength to tell Flint we were through; every day I backed down. Three times during that month we had sex, and I went home to ask God to forgive me and to give me the strength to regain control of my life.

Finally, in total desperation, I visited one of the women on the Campus Life staff and poured out my story. She listened to it all without saying a word. When I finished she said, "Jennifer, I don't think God wants you to regain control of your life."

I didn't understand, but she continued, "God wants you to give *him* control."

So that's what I did. Right there I prayed and told God that my life—all of it—was his. The next day I drove to Flint's house. He was going out just as I drove up. My legs felt a little shaky, so I didn't get out of my car. I told him I'd come to let him know that I didn't want to hurt him, but that our relationship was over.

He started his old speech about loving and needing me. I drove off while he was still talking. He called later that day and invited me over to his house to talk about it. I told him there was no use discussing it; my decision was final. When I tried to explain my reasons, he hung up.

I went up to my room and wrote Flint a six-page letter, telling him what had happened to me. I told him I'd started a new relationship—with God—and this one was serious from the start.

YOUR TURN

Stop Signs

My relationship with _____ went bad because

_____

Signs a person should break up with his/her boyfriend/girlfriend
are

_____

_____

If sex is a problem, what steps can you take to make it less of a
problem?

_____

_____

My sexual standards:

_____

_____

_____

_____

If You Need Forgiveness

If you need forgiveness. There's something about sex that affects us to the very core. We give a very important part of ourselves away in an intimacy that affects us deeply. As one writer put it, "Once you've given yourself away, it's hard to take yourself back." But what if you've given yourself completely, time and time again? Can you ever recover the scattered fragments? If you have given yourself away, there's hope. The same God that says sex is to be reserved for marriage offers a cure: forgiveness. Coming to Jesus, confessing your sin (agreeing with God that your action was wrong), resolving to change your ways, and asking for new strength to carry out that resolve—this is how you receive forgiveness and power to overcome temptation.

If you need forgiveness, take out a Bible and read 1 John 1:8–10. Confess your sin and ask for forgiveness and the strength to start afresh. (Warning: You may have to break up with your boyfriend/girlfriend. Most people find it almost impossible to go backward in a relationship once they've gotten involved physically. The only way this can be done is when *both people agree* to avoid any physical contact except for casual hand-holding until they get things well under control. Most couples can't or won't do this. That's why the best way to make a fresh start usually is to break up.)

Sometimes guilt feelings remain, even though you've asked forgiveness. If you still feel guilty after confessing your sin, remember that you also need to forgive yourself. Record your request for forgiveness in your journal: "I confessed my sin and received God's forgiveness on [date]. According to 1 John 1:8–10, God has forgiven me; therefore I also forgive myself and give my body to God as a living sacrifice" (see Rom. 12:1).

You might also want to copy down the following Scripture in your journal: "The Lord is compassionate and gracious, slow to anger, abounding in love. He will not always accuse, nor will he harbor his anger forever; he does not treat us as our sins deserve or repay us according to our iniquities. For as high as the heavens are above the earth, so great is his love for those who fear him; as far as the east is from the west, so far has he removed our transgressions from us" (Ps. 103:8–12).

memory verse

Struggles with Parents

Dr. Penny Smith

We couldn't leave this section without a word about the people who have influenced you most: Your parents. These are the years you are becoming your own person, and the transition is not always easy. In this article, Dr. Penny Smith talks about how to survive.

We psychiatrists see an unusual side of life, one where the problems often are exaggerated. Some kids who come to see me blurt out feelings that they have never in their lives told anyone. Others are so scared and shy at first that I can't get them to say a complete sentence. It's pretty rare for a teenager to come to me on his own. Usually Mom or Dad has encouraged him, which automatically puts two strikes against me.

I see a variety of problems in teenagers, but almost all have one thing in common: They're all bloody, bandaged victims of the "War of Independence." That war is a conflict required of just about everyone who grows up, and usually it's waged against the parent. The battlefields change over the years. Now it's things like drugs and sexuality, whereas years ago hair length or skirt length set the grounds for conflict.

When I can bring a teenager to the place where he opens up, he usually says something like this: "Is there *any* way you can get my mom and dad to understand?" He's almost pleading. There's a brick wall ten feet thick between him and his parents. Unfortunately, I usually must reply, "Probably not. I doubt they'll ever understand." Parents have simply forgotten what it was like when they went through the "War of Independence."

It's too bad we have to use something like war to describe the process of gaining independence. It's really a natural growth process that we adults ought to learn to accept. Every person has to go through a stretching, expanding period when he finds his own identity apart from his parents. A little baby's life is totally dependent on his parents. Even through grade school and junior high, most of a kid's life is determined for him by others: teachers, parents, youth directors. They set rules for him, tell him what he should learn and believe, and what decisions he should make.

But suddenly, in a brief period, the kid has to prepare himself to make all his own decisions and find out who he is and what he wants to be like. No wonder the battlefield gets a little smoky sometimes. Can parents ever understand what kids are going through? Many are very wise and understanding and know how to handle signs of growth or independence. But the kids I counsel usually come from homes where the parents simply cannot cope with the situation and the kid feels totally trapped.

It's interesting that the Bible only records one event from Jesus' growing-up years. He was twelve years old, and went to the temple with his parents. His mother and father took off on the journey home, assuming Jesus was with them, but suddenly they found out he was missing. Frightened, and probably angry, they rushed back to the temple and saw Jesus calmly holding court with the scholars. Can't you just imagine Mary's anxiety: "Son, do you realize what you put me through? I was worried sick!" But Jesus understood the "War of Independence." He knew his parents would have to adjust to a new scene as he grew up, and he could handle situations like that.

Note Jesus' reaction. He didn't sulk or throw a tantrum; he obeyed his parents and went with them. By the time you're a teenager, your parents have been looking after you for thirteen years. You can't expect them to let go of those strings overnight. It takes time and understanding from both parties.

Psychologists who study teenagers are finding out there are large differences between the ways teenagers and adults think and respond. The teenager's brain undergoes dramatic changes. He begins to use his brain for what scientists call "formal operations." For the first time he can logically manipulate thought, and therefore, quite naturally, the teenager spends a lot of time inside his own head thinking, figuring things out. Parents, on the other hand, see their kid as being spacey and lazy.

But you have to understand where the parents are coming from: they're concerned with survival. What's on your dad's mind in a day? His job satisfaction, rising prices, insurance bills, planning for your college, tensions with your mother. Your mother's probably concerned with feeding you, raising your brothers and sisters, and taking care of relatives. If she works, her task is doubly complex. Plus, most parents are plain scared; they've probably never done cocaine or smoked pot, but they read in *Time* magazine about the high percentages of people who do. They read the statistics of kids who have sex, and of the hundreds or thousands of unwed mothers, and they're scared to death for you and your future.

These are some of the reasons I say, "No, I can't cross that communication barrier between you and your parents." I don't think there can be perfect, clear understanding between parents and teenagers. You're coming from two different backgrounds, and you're going through different sets of pressures and tensions. So, if you feel your parents don't understand you—relax. Join the millions. You probably don't understand your parents either.

Is the situation hopeless? I've seen too many happy families to believe that. I think the biggest lesson a kid can learn is to accept and care for his parents even when there's no communication. Too often when problems arise the teenager sulks, refuses to talk, or won't cooperate around the house. Maybe he starts acting deliberately rebellious, antagonizing his parents. That's a dead end. My advice is to keep on trying to be understanding even when you're not getting through to your parents.

It's funny to see the roles flip-flop in a family. I see teenagers with mothers or fathers who simply won't let them have any independence. This is especially a problem among single-parent homes. In many single-parent cases the kids are the main source of the parent's identity; that's a heavy burden for anyone, particularly a kid. In such cases, the parent can be acting more childish than the teenager. He or she may become irrational, overemotional, stubborn. It's almost pitiful.

I try to help the teenager understand that, right now, the parent is weak. Kids can affect their parents; they can change them, build them up. When was the last time you expressed interest in your dad's job or in your parents' friends? When was the last time you asked about their hobbies or the vacations they took before you came along? Kids can hold the key to their parents' sense of self-worth. Your parents have invested an awful lot in you—are they seeing any return on their investment?

Another point I try to get across to kids is that their parents will fail them. That's a revolutionary thought to most kids. Often the most rebellious kids who really hurt their parents are plagued with tremendous guilt feelings. It's been hammered into them all their life that their parents are always right, so when differences erupt they feel it's their fault. It's much more likely that it is a mutual problem.

When these kinds of conflicts occur, it's important to have other people to lean on. Friends at school can help, but it would be even better to have an adult you can trust and relate to as a friend.

I've spent a lot of time describing homes that don't seem to work very well. So what kinds of homes do work? The most important ingredient I've seen is unconditional love. A parent should communicate to his kids that he loves and accepts them, *regardless*. Fill in anything you want: Regardless of the kid running away, sinning grossly, rejecting everything the parent stands for—the teenager has to believe his parents will love him no matter what.

Jesus' parable of the Prodigal Son in Luke 15:11–32 is the best example I can use here. Only in the family can you find that kind of accepting, forgiving love. James Dobson, in his book *Hide and Seek*, describes how a person rates in our society. He says society gives a gold coin of self-respect if you're beautiful; you get a silver coin if you have a lot of brains—that also gives you a sense of being valuable; you get a bronze coin for having money. The family should be directly opposed to that sort of value rating. You belong to your family simply because you exist. No matter how irritating you think your situation is, it's unlikely you'll find any other group in society that genuinely accepts you as freely as your family accepts you.

If your parents are wise enough to love you in spite of anything, you stand a chance of surviving the "War of Independence" without wounds. But remember, you, too, have a responsibility. You must love and accept your parents no matter what. No matter how boorish or unjust or cruel they appear to you, if you respond with love and maturity, God has promised to honor your actions. Who knows, if both parties—you and your parents—are showing unconditional love, you may be ready to sign a cease-fire.

YOUR TURN

Your Inheritance

Mother's Attributes:
(Go ahead, describe her.)

_____

_____

_____

Father's Attributes:
(Go ahead, describe him.)

_____

_____

_____

Which ones did you inherit?

_____

_____

_____

Are any of these attributes on your like/dislike lists from page 23?

Time to catch up on your correspondence!

DEAR MOM,

One reason I appreciate you is that you have given me part of yourself. By that I mean

_____

_____

_____

_____

_____

DEAR DAD,

One reason I appreciate you is that you have given me part of yourself. By that I mean

_____

_____

_____

_____

_____

Spiritual

We have missed the full impact
of the Gospel if we have not discovered what it is to be ourselves, loved
by God, irreplaceable to his sight,
unique among our fellow human beings.

If you have anything valuable
to contribute to the world, it will
come through the expression of your
own personality—that single spark
of divinity that sets you off and
makes you different from every
other living creature.

(Bruce Barton)

A Personal Relationship with God

Tim Stafford

A "personal relationship" with God. I kept quiet whenever anyone said that because, though I was a Christian, I wasn't sure I had a personal relationship with God.

When people used that phrase, it sounded as though they had an inside deal, a sort of hotline to heaven. For example, when I was trying to quit a job, my Christian boss was absolutely confident that I was doing the wrong thing. He sat me down and told me that God didn't want me to quit. "I was on my knees talking to God for three solid hours last night," he said, "and God definitely spoke to me. He told me you weren't supposed to quit this job." I countered by telling him that I hadn't gotten that message from God.

"But were you praying for three solid hours?" he pressed. "Has God told you you're supposed to quit?" I had to say no.

Personally, I don't hear voices. There have been occasions when I believe God firmly guided me away from one thing and toward another, but that makes my relationship more like an acquaintance—he doesn't guide me so directly very often. And I never hear voices.

In describing their personal relationship, some people also describe a great peace inside. "In the Garden," a beautiful hymn about prayer, expresses this well: "And he walks with me, and he talks with me, and he tells me I am his own. And the joy we share as we tarry there, none other has ever known."

For me, sometimes, it *is* a little like that—but only sporadically. More often, praying is hard work. It's something I know I should do but most days it doesn't produce a warm glow. So if a personal relationship with Christ is made up of warm feelings and direct communication, I can't claim to have a very good one.

What made me really nervous was the way some people would hint that all "real" Christians had their kind of warm, personal relationship with God. Inside me, a lot of guilt began to grow. Wasn't I a "real" Christian? Then why, no matter how much I cried out to God (and I can remember some particularly agonizing times when I asked God for just one word of reassurance) didn't I get that personal relationship I looked for? God wasn't as close as my roommate. He wasn't even as close as my grandfather. Only once in a while, when I wasn't looking for it, did God surprise me and seem to come very close.

I didn't become more comfortable with the phrase "personal relationship" overnight. It took a long time for me to realize that there actually *was* something very personal about my relationship with God—something that had always been there.

What I think we should mean when we say we have a personal relationship with God is this: God is a person, not an institution, idea, ideal, or principle. He is a person; all of his nature was expressed in Jesus Christ, a person who walked, talked, ate dinner, and had friends.

I am a person, too—not a dream, not a machine, not an animal, not a body or a spirit only.

Now how, as a person, do I relate? I may write letters or talk with someone over the phone. But I don't necessarily relate to others as a buddy. Factors such as age or social differences may keep a relationship rather formal. Still, certain things do happen when people relate:

1. *Persons communicate ideas.* My point of view is gradually, subtly affected by others. Likewise, God communicates ideas, helping me to understand his way of thinking.

2. *Persons affect each other through love and encouragement.* I can love my car to death, but I can't make it run any better. When I love another person, however, I do help that person "run better." God affects me tremendously, gradually, by the amazing way he loves me.

3. *When a person is loved, he frequently begins to model*

his life after the one who loves him. My parents have loved me longer and harder than anyone else, and it's amazing how, more and more, I find their traits in me. When my friends love me, I find myself starting to talk like them and go to the same places they like. So my relationship with God is personal in that I model myself after him; I begin to want to be like Jesus.

4. *When a person gives advice to a friend, he does it politely.* I don't force friends to respond to my suggestions, even if I'm quite sure I'm right. That is true of God, as well. He never forces himself or his ideas on me. He is gentle, and, as a gentleman, he respects my freedom.

5. *Persons help each other deal with trouble.* Likewise, God helps me just that way.

So when I say I have a personal relationship with God, I mean this: God is a person and I treat him that way. I am a person and God treats me that way.

It does not necessarily mean that we communicate in a conversation. Moses did, apparently, but I don't. I talk, believing that God is listening; so far he has not talked back, though sometimes he has used my feelings and thoughts to point me in a different direction than I was ready to go. He has done most of his talking to me through the Bible.

I have to admit, I would like it better if I could see God and have a genuine conversation with him. I wish I didn't have to muster up faith to believe that he is constantly with me; I would like him to be obvious. But evidently that doesn't matter as much as I think. What matters is that I learn to believe God even when it's not obvious that he cares. What matters is that I allow him, as an unspeakably loving and completely wise person, to affect me, a person who needs that love and wisdom. He is doing that, and that is why I am no longer nervous about the phrase "personal relationship."

Make no mistake: I am not content. I would like to have a conversation with God. I would like to be with him "physically," whatever that would mean. I would like it if his love were absolutely, unshakably obvious.

Someday, I believe, it will be.

YOUR TURN

Who Is God, Anyway?

Look up the following list of Bible images, then explain in your journal what each image means to you and why you need that kind of relationship with God. (I have done the first one to give you an example of what you should do.)

God is my Guide: Psalm 31:3; 48:14; Isaiah 58:11; John 16:13. *I have some important decisions coming up, and I need guidance on which way to go. I need to ask God to show me what's best. It's good to know he will be my guide.*

God is my Father (Daddy): Matthew 6:9; Romans 8:15; Ephesians 3:14–15.

_____

_____

God is my Counselor, Comforter: Psalm 7:8–11; Isaiah 9:6; John 14:16.

_____

_____

God is my Teacher: Psalm 32:8; Isaiah 2:3; John 3:2; 14:26.

_____

_____

God is my Judge: Genesis 18:25; Psalm 7:8–11; Isaiah 33:22; Revelation 19:11.

God is my Friend: Proverbs 18:24; Matthew 11:19; John 15:15.

God is my Helper: Psalm 54:4; Hebrews 13:6.

God is my Mother: Isaiah 66:13; Matthew 23:37.

God is my Husband: Isaiah 54:5; Revelation 21:2.

God is my Shepherd: Psalm 23; John 10:11–16.

Losing Yourself

Gregg Lewis

God holds the true key to who you are. He is the one who can show you your weaknesses and strengths, and he is the one who can even turn your weaknesses into strengths (2 Cor. 12:7–10). He is the one who chose your genetic structure (Ps. 139:13), who knows when you get up and when you go to bed every day, and all that you do in between (Ps. 139).

But Jesus is more than all this. He doesn't just help you do what you already want to do. Didn't Jesus say, "Whoever finds his life will lose it, and whoever loses his life for my sake will find it" (Matt. 10:39)? How does that fit with "finding yourself," or "defining your self-image"? Is it wrong to have concentrated on yourself as intensely as you have done so far in this book? Shouldn't you put God first and seek to serve him by doing "religious" things? The following two articles put this teaching by Jesus into perspective.

The more I got to know Scott, the harder time I had liking the guy. He was one of those self-centered people who failed to realize others weren't fascinated by every detail in his life. He'd tell me stories about what he'd done in baseball practice the week before, complete with play-by-play commentary on the "unbelievable" curve he'd lined off the pitcher's foot and the "spectacular" diving catch he'd made into the first-base stands. He'd describe this great pizza place where he and his buddies usually met, how much they'd eat, and who they'd talk to. He'd recount a dozen classroom stories, including all the smart remarks he'd made to crack up his friends. Then there were the stories about girls. He never stopped talking about his exploits.

Obviously, all the talk was just a cover-up for Scott's insecurity. But knowing that didn't make him any easier to like.

We lived in different towns, but because our parents were friends our families got together several times a year. So, like him or not, I spent a lot of time with Scott through high school. We shared many of the same interests and could have become close friends. But we never did. Scott was so wrapped up in himself I doubt if he had a real friendship with anyone. In all his talking, I don't remember him once asking about anything happening in my life.

When I think of people with whom it's impossible to be friends, I also remember Carole. I hadn't thought of her since high school graduation until I noticed her picture on a recent flip-through of an old annual. I had to look up her name. She wasn't bad looking; you could even have called her "cute." She pulled better-than-average grades. But the one thing that stands out in my mind about Carole was her shyness.

I half suspected she hid in her locker between classes to escape the people-crowded halls. She almost always slipped into class just before the final bell—her way of avoiding talk. I think she was absent every day an oral report was due.

Carole and I occasionally rode the same bus to school, so I tried to be friendly. But every time I began a conversation she looked as if she were going to be ill. So I quit trying.

I felt sorry for Carole in a way I didn't feel sorry for Scott, but I have since come to the conclusion that they both had the same basic problem: Self-centeredness. They reacted in opposite extremes, but they both were so concerned about themselves and how they appeared to other people that they were incapable of forming meaningful relationships.

Over the past few years, I've run across a number of people as emotionally crippled by self-centeredness as Scott and Carole. And I always feel a little uncomfortable, perhaps even a little superior, as I say to myself, "I'm glad I don't have their problem."

And yet, I do. I may not be a boring braggart or a withered

wallflower, but my self-centeredness shows up in other ways. When I'm introduced to someone the first time, I'm often so preoccupied with making a good impression and wondering what he or she thinks of me that I don't catch the person's name. I've been working on that, but too often I still find myself talking to nameless strangers only two minutes after we've been introduced.

My self-centeredness also smacks me in the face when I stop to realize how little thought and concern I invest in needs of other people. Most days I spend more time trying to decide whether to have a Big Mac or Quarter Pounder than thinking about the millions of undernourished people in the world; I put more thought into planning my weekend entertainment than looking for a lonely person to befriend; I expend more effort arguing my point of view than listening to someone else's problems.

These things bother me, though if I wanted to shrug them off I could easily blame my self-centeredness on the world in which I live. It seems everyone is out to sell me on my importance. TV commercials brainwash me with blaring compliments: "You deserve a break today . . ." and "You never looked so good." Everyone nods in supportive understanding at the phrase, "I just gotta do my own thing." Best-sellers tell me how to assert myself and win what I want by intimidation. One book even explains *How to Be Your Own Best Friend.*

I can hear the summary of our culture's message from psychologists, teachers, and the media, and friends who all advise: *"You have to find yourself."* That's true, to a certain extent. I've seen people who never understand and accept themselves—they often end up like Scott or Carole, or worse. So finding myself and developing an accurate, healthy self-image *is* a key to relating to other people. It affects every area of my life. Finding myself is terribly important.

And yet I struggle with this as a Christian because it seems to contradict Jesus' statement, "The person who finds his life will lose it; he who loses his life for my sake will find it."

Sometimes I wish Jesus hadn't said that, but he did. The Bible records it four times—more often than anything else Jesus said. So it must be important. But what did he mean? How could losing my life result in finding it? Before I understood that verse I had to do away with a couple common misconceptions about what it teaches. In essence, I had to realize what Jesus didn't mean.

First, Jesus wasn't merely talking about acts of heroism: a soldier diving onto a grenade to save his squad; a fireman dying of burns after carrying an invalid from a blazing house; a young mother throwing herself into the street to knock her child away just before a speeding car ends her own life. Jesus was talking about more than life-sacrificing heroics.

Second, when Jesus said, "He who loses his life for my sake will find it," he wasn't promising some sort of eternal consolation prize. He wasn't offering a trade-off of future reward for present unhappiness.

For a while I thought that was what Jesus meant; if I did what God wanted, my present life would be unpleasant but he'd somehow make it up to me later. That kind of thinking kept me away from God for a few years. I decided I'd become a Christian some day, but I just wasn't ready to lose my life and have to wait until eternity to find it again. I wanted to experience the good things in life now—find myself, develop my potential. I figured I'd get my life headed in the direction I wanted by making all the crucial decisions myself concerning college major, career, and wife. Then, after I'd gotten so much momentum built up that God wouldn't be able to get in the way of my plans, I would become a Christian.

But things didn't turn out that way. By my first year in college I felt fearfully uncertain about my future. The "good things in life" that I'd wanted to experience didn't seem so good. I didn't like myself for being a hypocrite in front of my parents and friends who thought I was a Christian. The girl I was dating wasn't someone I wanted to marry. I was making a mess of everything.

So I finally turned to God and told him I was sorry, that I was blowing my life, and I needed Jesus to take over. That was my first step in learning what Jesus meant with his lose-life/find-life riddle. In a sense, my decision to become a Christian was a decision to lose my life. I gave up control—but the result was not the dreary martyrdom I'd dreaded. The feeling was closer to relief.

Admitting I needed God's help took a lot of pressure off me. After all, if I'm willing to tell God I've failed, that I've sinned, then there's nothing left to hide. And if he's accepted me and taken over my life, I shouldn't have to worry about proving myself to other people. I say shouldn't have to because asking God's help didn't mean the immediate end of all my self-centeredness. Becoming a Christian *is* part of the answer to Jesus' lose-self/find-self teaching, but it's only the beginning.

The rest takes place today, tomorrow, every day I live as a Christian. If I've truly lost my life by giving it up to Jesus, then I ought to be living and making decisions based on his standards and teaching, not my own preferences.

That often requires sacrifice: visiting a sick friend when I'd rather spend the evening at a movie or a ball game; doing what my dad asks without pointing out that my brother already left without doing his chores; getting to know a new student in the library when I'd prefer to be at a tableful of friends. It may even mean making a greater effort to reach out and relate to people like Scott and Carole.

Sometimes it seems these little day-to-day sacrifices of putting other people first are harder than noble acts of heroism would be. Some days I don't feel like sacrificing at all; I'd sooner hurl myself in front of someone being shot than give up my lunch hour to help a friend. This daily process of losing myself takes perseverance to become a habit.

Yet I don't want to imply that living a Christian life of daily sacrifice is a tedious chore. On the contrary, when Jesus says those who lose life will find life, he's promising a full, contented, satisfied life.

I've seen proof. The most contented, satisfied, and cheerful people I've known are the most giving, generous, and selfless people.

How can I find my life by losing it? It's a riddle that makes sense. God made me. He knows my weaknesses and strengths. It naturally follows that if I give up my feeble efforts at self-centered control and let him take charge, God will show me both what I can do and who I am.

I'll find myself. And I'll find my life.

True Spirituality

Jay Kesler

He came up to me after I was done speaking, with that look of sublime certainty in his eye. He didn't think I was very spiritual. He was hoping to help me out.

So I said, "Will you pray for me?" and I bowed my head. He was taken aback a little, but he did pray, and I thanked him.

Then I began to probe him a little on what his idea of spirituality was. Soon it was obvious that his was a little different from mine. I was asking him, "Besides praying that the Holy Spirit will bless us by giving us warm feelings and cozy groups to share in, isn't it spiritual to pray that he'll show us down-and-out people we can help? Is there a widow on your block whose lawn you could mow? Are there lonely people at school you could befriend? Does your church have missionaries overseas for whom you could concentrate on praying? Are you using your money to help anybody?" He didn't really think of those things as "spiritual."

Every Christian wants to be "spiritual," but just what does it mean? The first definition that comes to mind might be "being in touch with God." But how do you measure that? By good feelings? By the number of people with whom you've shared Christ? How does a person go about being "in touch with God?"

One very popular explanation of spirituality today seems to be "the more removed from the world you are, the more your mind is constantly on spiritual things, and the more spiritual you are." Translated into the way other people see Christians, this means "the more weird you are, the better Christian you must be." It's the kind of definition that brought about the sentence, "He's so heavenly minded he's no earthly good."

I don't want to be overly critical. I once believed in this kind of spirituality myself, but we need to see beyond it. Does real spirituality only care about souls? Does it make the earth just one big train station, a place where people decide whether they'll get on the train bound for heaven? That's the way "otherworldly" spirituality tends to see it. In this view, the world is a place to be escaped as soon as possible. We shouldn't use our minds; that's of no use to God. The only thing we should read is the Bible.

There used to be a commune in California where only the leader could read anything besides the Bible. He read the newspaper each day so he could report to the group on what Bible prophecies were fulfilled.

Sports, of course, are pointless if that's your definition of spirituality. So are art, beauty, ecology, politics—you name it. Why should we pay attention to them if the whole point of life is to get off the earth, not stay on it? We want to get away from these minds that hang us up with constant questions and doubts, away from these bodies that are always making us lustful or sleepy when we're praying.

Most Christians, I think, go through at least a stage where they believe this kind of theology. I certainly did. Why? Because most of us have mixed feelings about life. The world is a confusing, demanding, difficult place to live in. It's hostile to us. We want to put signs on it that read Danger, Keep Away. Then we call ourselves "spiritual."

WAS JESUS SPIRITUAL?

But when you read the Bible, you have a hard time holding that view. Jesus was a very earthly man who was criticized for going to too many parties with the wrong kind of people. When he prayed his last prayer for the disciples in John 17 he specifically said, "I'm not asking you to take them out of the world."

Also, if the world is just something we're trying to get away from, why did God look at it after he'd made it and say, "It is very good"?

God isn't inefficient. If all he cared about were our souls, it would have been much simpler to make us fuzzy gray balls floating in space. No minds, no real bodies, no personalities, just "souls." Why go to the trouble of making us so complicated?

So true spirituality is bigger than just souls and praying and Bible reading—but how can we define it?

The definition of spirituality that I support came to me years ago, in the early days of Youth for Christ, when I was asking a different kind of question. What was hitting us at YFC then was the fact that people between thirteen and nineteen are in a very special position. They're adults in many ways, and yet they're still living under other people's authority—that of their parents, teachers, coaches, and bosses. What does the Bible have to say to their situation?

Really, it doesn't say much. Mostly it deals with men and women who are fully adults. You do have Mary pregnant at thirteen or fourteen, but in her society she was considered fully mature, ready for the responsibility of being an adult.

Then we noticed this statement in Luke 2:52 about Jesus' boyhood: "And Jesus grew in wisdom and stature, and in favor with God and men."

That statement contains everything we know about Jesus from the time he turned twelve to the time of his baptism, at the age of thirty, by John the Baptist. Considering how Jesus turned out, those years of development must have been on target.

As those of us at Youth for Christ read this verse over, we thought it might give some clues to a young person's spirituality. So we looked at it more carefully, to see the various components. First we noticed that Jesus grew in wisdom—that's the sphere of the mind. He also grew in stature—in other words, his body was growing. Finally, he grew in favor with God and men—the spiritual and social dimensions were both well-adjusted; he got along with God and with his peers.

We looked at these four areas—mental, physical, spiritual, and social—and saw that they all were important. It wasn't enough to grow only in relationship to God—you also had to grow in relationship to your friends. You had to grow physically and mentally. Why? Because Jesus did.

Later I noticed a similarity in another crucial passage,

Romans 12:1–2. Paul writes: "I urge you, brothers, in view of God's mercy, to offer your bodies [physical] as living sacrifices, holy and pleasing to God—this is your spiritual act of worship. Do not conform any longer to the pattern of this world [social], but be transformed by the renewing of your mind [mental]. Then you will be able to test and approve what God's will is [spiritual]—his good, pleasing and perfect will."

From these verses came the concept of "the balanced life": When you remember these four areas, we said, it will help you keep a healthy perspective on yourself. Everyone probably will emphasize one of these areas more than the others: a jock will emphasize the physical, a genius will emphasize the mental, etc. But if all these areas show development, you will be a balanced, healthy person. That's why in Campus Life we still refer to the balanced life. We don't think any of these areas should be left out.

WAS BEETHOVEN BALANCED?

I've had kids come up to me and say, "Was Beethoven balanced? Seems to me that the people who really accomplish great things are imbalanced; they're driven in one direction. What you're saying seems to make everyone normal, healthy—and bland."

I can't deny that a lot of the greatest men and women of history were not normal, but eccentric. A lot of them weren't easy to get along with. They had such deep interest in one area that they couldn't pay attention to anything else.

I wonder, what made them eccentric? Were they eccentric because they chose to be? Did Beethoven choose to suffer emotionally? Or was he forced into that role by people who couldn't take the way he broke through all the old musical categories? A lot of the great writers and musicians, it seems to me, are saying things so true that people can't listen to them. Still, the great artist must tell the truth; he can't compromise it. So he ends up driven into eccentricity by other people. He didn't necessarily have to be that way to be creative.

Let's make a distinction here. There are lots of "driven" people around. Some great men, like Gandhi or Martin Luther King, Jr., were driven by truly great compassion and ideals. Others, like Hitler, were driven by hatred and a lust for power. There's nothing great about being driven. It all depends on what you're driven by.

You could say Jesus Christ was as eccentric as any man who lived. Why couldn't he forget his obsession about God? Why not settle down in Nazareth, get married, and calm down? He couldn't because he, too, was driven—driven by the love of God and the desire to do his will. So when the Spirit led Jesus into his public ministry, he responded. There was no compromise.

But that didn't make him "imbalanced" in the sense I mean here. Since God wanted him to serve him in that unique way, it was the only way he could be truly balanced. He didn't neglect the physical, the social, or the mental areas of life. He had friends. He was far from anti-intellectual. He wasn't a weakling. He just followed the will of God. That kind of "being driven" never causes imbalance.

If you hope to be great, what better model of success is there than Christ? Of course, Jesus didn't try to be on top. He wouldn't run over his rivals; in fact, he said, "Love your enemies." He was nonviolent. He didn't publicize himself; when he did something stupendous, most of the time he'd instruct the witness not to tell anyone.

The Roman Empire was hardly an age for becoming famous that way. The empire was the age of the conquering Caesars—but how many of those fierce Roman emperors can you name? They're just half-forgotten names in a history book. Jesus, the insignificant, unpublicized itinerant Preacher, is certainly the most famous man who ever lived.

TRUE SPIRITUALITY

So far, I've mentioned the spiritual as though it were one-fourth of a balanced life; sort of a holy little room in your insides.

That isn't really an accurate picture.

The real truth is more startling, more removed from the stereotyped "religious" answer. The spiritual dimension is the point at which all the other dimensions of life—the mental, physical, and social—are committed to God. There is no spiritual dimension to life where there aren't mental, physical, or social dimensions as well. Spirituality doesn't happen in a vacuum.

This is where commitment takes on real meaning. When someone becomes a Christian, we say he "commits himself to Christ," but what does that mean? Does it imply a little ceremony in church where you stand up and walk down the aisle? Or does it imply that you pray certain words?

No, it means the commitment of each area of life to God. God wants us, Paul says in Romans 12, to present our bodies as a living sacrifice to him. The emphasis is on the *living*. He isn't interested in human sacrifice, as so many pagan religions have thought. He wants living sacrifices: people who eat, play, talk, think, and make friends in a way that is consciously committed to God. That's what spirituality is about.

Be aware, however, that the devil also wants living sacrifices. He wants you to be irresponsible in the way you act. He wants you to eat, play, talk, think, and make friends *his* way. So there is a constant battle going on. You're the one who decides which side you'll be on.

God wants you to commit your body to him. That means, first of all, that you shouldn't abuse your body. Smoking is a lousy idea. Being out of shape or overweight is a bad idea. Drugs and drunkenness are bad ideas. Why? Because they're not responsible uses of your body. They're not wrong because God drew up some arbitrary lists of things he wanted to take away from us. They're wrong because they're against the positive act of committing your body to Christ.

Do you realize that playing football can be spiritual exercise? It can be, because God is interested in your body. Do you get enough sleep and eat the right food in preparation for playing a sport? Do you make sure you will be able to put your best efforts, physically and emotionally, into the game? The Devil wants you to be irresponsible; God wants you to be responsible.

It goes even further than that. You can misuse your body subtly. A girl can use her body irresponsibly to manipulate and lead guys around. That's not a responsible use of her body, because it denies her full personhood (not to mention the damage to the guys involved).

A guy can get infatuated with his body. He can care for nothing except how tremendous an athlete he is. He can groom his body as though there were no tomorrow. But that is irresponsible, too—not because being a good athlete is wrong, but because God made us to be more than just well-built bodies. Fitness isn't an end in itself.

How about your minds? I'd say the biggest lack of spirituality in the realm of the mind stems from laziness. People don't use their minds fully. For some reason Christians often are more guilty of this than other people, as though being ignorant were somehow spiritual. I look around a room of Christian kids and I wonder, *Could there be a cure for cancer in this room? Could there be a great piece of music? Could there be a novel as great as* War and Peace?

But it won't happen if you don't give your mind to God. Where do you think Jonas Salk, who discovered the vaccine for polio, would be if he had had your attitude in chemistry?

What are you letting your mind absorb? Is it soaking up a lot of TV shows? Or pornography? Or is it becoming saturated with the Word of God?

There are whole other areas of the mind to give to God. How about your thoughts concerning the opposite sex? Do you think of people selfishly, in terms of what they have to offer you or what you can get from them? Or do your thoughts center on how you can responsibly show them love?

Of course, this spills over into the whole area of relationships. These need to be given to God, too. You should aim for the kind of relationships that reflect God's love. You shouldn't only include the beautiful people in your friendships. All people are God's children whether they're lovely to look at or not.

This area can have subtle challenges, too. Suppose you have a close group of friends. You value these friends. You value the closeness of the group. Then suppose someone new starts hanging around the fringe of the group. How do you react? If you're irresponsible, you think of ways to protect your status and position in your group. You worry about losing the closeness of your little group. But if you've committed your social life to God, you should welcome this person. Trust God to take care of your need for friendship and look for opportunities to befriend people.

These kinds of commitment—physical, mental, and social—go on and on. There isn't any end. The more you experience life, the more you will see areas of life you will need to give to God. Things you wouldn't have thought had anything to do with God will become great areas for spiritual growth.

Suppose you live to be eighty-five or ninety. By that time you will probably have given just about everything in your life to God.

Imagine Fred, eighty-five years old, riding along in his car with Maude, his wife. In the car in front of them there are two teenagers snuggled up to one another. The girl is kind of nibbling the guy's ear, and he's got his arm around her. Old Fred gets all riled up. He turns to Maude and says, "Maude, just look at those disgusting kids. Kids just aren't like we were. They have smutty minds. Why aren't they interested in doing things like we did when we were young, like going to church every night of the week, and listening to two-hour sermons, and praying for three hours at a time? It's disgusting."

Maude leans over and says kind of sweetly, "Fred, remember when we were going together, and that time we parked out by the river . . . ?"

Fred says, "I don't remember anything of the kind!" Then he drives grumpily along muttering about how the kids are going to the dogs.

That night old Fred doesn't sleep too well; he just lies in bed thinking about those kids, and he realizes he was wrong. So he prays, "God, I'm sorry I judged those kids. Help me to mind my own business and to have an open mind about things." Then he turns over and goes to sleep. It's really beautiful, because Fred, at eighty-five, is still finding areas of his life he can give to God.

This is what spirituality is all about: presenting ourselves as *living* sacrifices to God. It's committing our lives to God; it's being aware that God is involved in our lives and that he is offering his grace and forgiveness.

This kind of spirituality keeps going and growing. It doesn't wear out. On the other hand, that narrow box of "spirituality" that is divorced from everything else soon becomes irrelevant, just a habit or an emotional release you use occasionally. True spirituality goes on forever.

YOUR TURN

Like God

"God created man in his own image, in the image of God he created him; male and female he created them" (Gen. 1:27).

Look up the verses and write the answers in.

1 John 4:16 shows that God is *love. I am like God when I go out of my way to help my little brother Ricky with his homework.*

Psalm 36:5 shows that God is _____

I am like God when _____

Psalm 145:17 shows that God is _____

I am like God when _____

Psalm 103:8 shows that God is _____

I am like God when _____

John 15:11 shows that God is _____

I am like God when _____

Making (Spiritual) Changes

Jim Long

Jay Kesler is right when he says that being spiritual affects every area of your life. You take the power of God that is available to you and apply it to each aspect of your life. How can this be done? Check out the next article, in which Jim Long shares practical advice from the Bible on this very subject.

OK. There are things that are out of your control. You can't make yourself shorter. You can't zap yourself into a genius. You can't force the world to fall all over you in awe. There are certain things that only God can change, and, for reasons that remain a mystery, he may not change what you want him to change—but that's only half the story.

The other half is this: *You have more control over yourself than you may imagine.* You can be a better you. You have control. So what's holding you back?

Sometimes we get the funny idea that we can't control our thoughts. We can. Read this: "The weapons we fight with are not the weapons of the world. On the contrary, they have divine power to demolish strongholds. We demolish arguments and every pretension that sets itself up against the knowledge of God, and we take captive every thought to make it obedient to Christ" (2 Cor. 10:4–5).

Control. Over thoughts. We have it.

"Whatever is true, whatever is noble, whatever is right, whatever is pure, whatever is lovely, whatever is admirable—if anything is excellent or praiseworthy—think about such things" (Phil. 4:8).

We can control our thoughts. But when I say, "You have control over your mind," I mean more than moral control. I mean the control illustrated in the old axiom: "Your head is your house. Furnish it." You have your limitations, but you *can* improve yourself intellectually.

Read. Study. Think. Sharpen your reasoning skills. Broaden your mental horizons. Make your brain a better place.

You can.

You have control.

Your clock could stop today. Breath by breath, life is a gift.

Or *you* could cut things short—an unwise and unproductive option. Some people practice slow-motion suicide: drugs, alcohol, unbridled sex. Over the long haul, these things hurt. Sometimes they even hurt deeply after the "short haul." But you don't have to choose behavior that hurts you. You have control.

"Do you not know that your body is a temple of the Holy Spirit, who is in you, whom you have received from God? You are not your own; you were bought at a price. Therefore honor God with your body" (1 Cor. 6:19–20).

Have you considered that it is a gift from God that you can tone your muscles through exercise, that you can improve your health and extend your life through a proper diet, that you can stay healthy through good hygiene?

You have control.

You may not instantaneously turn perfect, but you can know God better.

True: "'God opposes the proud but gives grace to the humble.' Submit yourselves, then, to God. Resist the devil, and he will flee from you. Come near to God and he will come near to you" (James 4:6–8).

True: "For it is God who works in you to will and to act according to his good purpose" (Phil. 2:13). God himself strengthens your faith as he works within you.

Also true: You have responsibility. And control. "Make every effort to add to your faith goodness; and to goodness, knowledge; and to knowledge, self-control; and to self-control, perseverance; and to perseverance, godliness; and to godliness, brotherly kindness; and to brotherly kindness, love. For if you possess these qualities in increasing measure, they will keep you from being ineffective and unproductive in your knowledge of our Lord Jesus Christ. . . . If you do these things, you will never fall" (2 Peter 1:5–8, 10).

You can have a stronger faith by adding these characteristics from Scripture:

Goodness (be nice)

Knowledge (read the Bible)

Self-control (give temptation the boot)

Perseverance (be patient)

Godliness (act like God—be holy)

Brotherly kindness (be gentle)

Love (be unselfish and giving)

Your life can look more like Jesus' life. A lot more.

You have control.

I am tempted to say, "You have control over your personality." And if I did, I would be partly correct. People may disagree over how much control. So let's not be technical. Let's just say this: "You can be more likable."

Or think of it this way: "You have control over your friends." I do not mean that you manipulate them or change their actions, thoughts, or feelings—though this sometimes happens. What I do mean is that you can change yourself and make yourself a better friend, a more pleasant person, and someone who is nice to be around.

You can't force people to like you—forceful efforts of this kind almost always fail—but you do have control over your friendliness. As you become a loving, caring person, something happens within your friends, too. "Love is patient, love is kind. It does not envy, it does not boast, it is not proud. It is not rude, it is not self-seeking, it is not easily angered, it keeps no record of wrongs. Love does not delight in evil but rejoices with the truth. It always protects, always trusts, always hopes, always perseveres. Love never fails" (1 Cor. 13:4–8).

You'd like to have friends who cared like that.

So be a friend who cares like that.

You can.

You have control.

YOUR TURN

Self-Inspection

I would evaluate myself in these areas as follows:

Knowledge   1 _____ 5 _____ 10

Self-Control   1 _____ 5 _____ 10

Perseverance   1 _____ 5 _____ 10

Godliness   1 _____ 5 _____ 10

Kindness   1 _____ 5 _____ 10

Love   1 _____ 5 _____ 10

Joy   1 _____ 5 _____ 10

Peace   1 _____ 5 _____ 10

Patience   1 _____ 5 _____ 10

The area I would most like to grow in is _____

because _____

Who Am I? Who Can I Become?

Jim Long

You will not remain as you are today. You will grow and change, becoming more God's person as you follow him. This process you have started in this book, the process of discovering who you are, will continue all your life.

Jim Long captures this sense of being and becoming more of who we are in this chapter. As you read it, remember that growth is a process. *It takes time, and that is part of the plan. So relax, enjoy what you've become so far, and dream a little about what you'd like to become.*

I have this image of what I should have been. Yesterday. Years ago.

Yesterday my temper flared Why? There was no adequate reason, but unkind words gushed out. I couldn't hold them back. And that torrent surged over my friend, who stood dumbfounded, wondering what could possibly have caused this.

I wondered, too.

"Stop!" I wanted to shout to myself. "You've said enough. Too much. You're not making sense." But I bumbled on in my rage, blurting nonsense that I regretted even as I said it.

Anger is like that.

And I have this image of what I should have been yesterday, years ago: forgiving, kind, patient.

Yet, frustrated, I realize that my outburst of anger was not one fault among many virtues, but that my life's few lonely virtues stood surrounded by my many flaws. Or so it seemed to me. Yesterday. Years ago.

I stretched the truth (I lied). I wallowed in ingratitude. I cheated on my final. I took advantage of my special friend so that we both felt shame. I blasted my father with fiery words. (Anger again.)

All this. And yet somehow, yesterday, I was forgiven. God, I discovered, is quite willing to look beyond my failures, my twisted morals, and to call me "clean."

Why? Because of some faint spark of good within me? Or is it because—simply because of my friend Christ and what he did for me one yesterday, years ago? And is it because I reached out to accept the gift that my friend Christ came to give me new life?

"If anyone is in Christ, he is a new creation; the old has gone, the new has come! . . . God made him who had no sin to be sin for us, so that in him we might become the righteousness of God" (2 Cor. 5:17, 21).

I have this image of what I should be. Today. Right now. But I am so aware of how far short I fall of even my minimal expectations of myself. I am a long-distance runner who first tells himself, "I will complete the marathon within three hours," only to find during practice that I am unable, by my calculation, to break even the *four*-hour limit. So, determination overshadowed by discouragement, I readjust my goals. "I will at least complete the race," I tell myself, then add, with a faint smile of strained purpose, "within four and a half hours."

Perhaps I *will* approach the four-hour barrier—but I know, even if no one else ever suspects it, that I have adjusted my goal. And my performance suffers. Endurance lags.

I tell myself, "Today, I will be perfect. Today I will conquer my unkindness. I will overcome lies with costly honesty. I will unlock the secret of doing good, of thinking right. I will cross the moral finish line and crown my life with virtue. I will run the race, you might say, in less than three hours."

Then I turn to see my flagging performance, and I realize with bitter discouragement that I am fighting over and over again some of the same battles. Morally, I have broken my stride. The perfection I had dreamed of sprinting through with ease now becomes something I will never achieve.

I toy with the thought of readjusting my moral goals. If I can't attain perfection today, why humiliate myself by trying? If—again today—I must face my anger, if today I must mud-wrestle my ingratitude, if today I must brace myself against the incessant temptation to cheat, if today I must strain to win out over my impure thoughts . . . why keep trying?

If goodness must be so ridiculously elusive, perhaps I should redefine wrong itself. Perhaps I should be easier on myself—set realistic, attainable goals. Today, I will simply complete the race. Or, if not, I will stride—sulking, bruised, self-defeated—off the course. Today, I will just give up.

Then, on further thought, my own analogy strikes me. I do not complete a race by planting my feet on the starting line and then, at the crack of the gun, leaping the twenty-six miles in one bound to the finish line. Such an image is absurd, yet this is my self-imposed expectation: Today, every day, I *ought* to be able simply to leap, or at least sprint, my way to holy perfection.

So, daily I struggle with virtue, stride by excruciating stride. Through painful training, through uncompromising persistence, through agonizing endurance, I change my uncompleted marathon into a five-hour race, a four-hour success, a three-hour victory. Day by day, through my own effort, my moral life improves.

However, there is a flaw in this "run the race" image: It is incomplete. It tells only part of the story. If I were to run the moral race simply by the determination I could muster, I'd collapse, wheezing and sputtering. I need a coach, a trainer. No, more—I need a supernatural runner who can climb inside my skin, infuse me with holy stamina, and run out the many miles through my limbs.

"So I find this law at work: When I want to do good, evil is right there with me. For in my inner being I delight in God's law; but I see another law at work in the members of my body, waging war against the law of my mind and making me a prisoner of the law of sin at work within my members. What a wretched man I am! Who will rescue me from this body of death? Thanks be to God— through Jesus Christ our Lord!" (Rom. 7:21–25).

I have this image of what I can become. Tomorrow. Years from now.

Tomorrow, I will make it. I will achieve what my spirit has been aching for: I will be perfect. My morals will shine. I will shed anger like a snake sheds withered skin. Ingratitude will be pushed aside by deep and sincere thankfulness. Cheating will not penetrate my thoughts. Impurity will be unthinkable. And I will be glad to be so good; it won't seem prudish or prissy or weak.

Someday, some tomorrow, I will be truly good—and I will possess the virtue to know that I have not drummed up all this goodness on my own. I will know I have inherited it from the only One who was ever perfect in his yesterdays and todays—from my Father.

"How great is the love the Father has lavished on us, that we should be called children of God! And that is what we are! The reason the world does not know us is that it did not know him. Dear friends, now we are children of God, and what we will be has not yet been made known. But we know that when he appears, we shall be like him, for we shall see him as he is. Everyone who has this hope in him purifies himself, just as he is pure" (1 John 3:1–3).

YOUR TURN

Summing Up

Look back over the exercises you've done throughout this book. Have you learned anything about yourself? Do you have a more accurate picture of who you are at this moment in time? Write down some of the key things you've learned.

1. _____

2. _____

3. _____

4. _____

5. _____

Now think: What's the picture you'd like to see a year from now? Two years? Three? Write down some of the key changes you hope to see.

1. _____

2. _____

3. _____